ACTIVELY CARING FOR PEOPLE
POLICING

ACTIVELY CARING FOR PEOPLE
POLICING

Building Positive
POLICE/CITIZEN
Relations

E. SCOTT GELLER[1]
BOBBY KIPPER[2]

New York

ACTIVELY CARING FOR PEOPLE POLICING
Building Positive POLICE/CITIZEN *Relations*

Published in New York, New York, by Morgan James Publishing. Morgan James and The Entrepreneurial Publisher are trademarks of Morgan James, LLC. www.MorganJamesPublishing.com

The Morgan James Speakers Group can bring authors to your live event. For more information or to book an event visit The Morgan James Speakers Group at www.TheMorganJamesSpeakersGroup.com.

ISBN 978-1-68350-055-1 paperback
ISBN 978-1-68350-056-8 eBook
Library of Congress Control Number: 2016906590

Cover Design by:
Rachel Lopez
www.r2cdesign.com

Interior Design by:
Bonnie Bushman
The Whole Caboodle Graphic Design

Illustrations by:
George Wills
Blacksburg, VA

Shelfie

A **free** eBook edition is available with the purchase of this print book.

CLEARLY PRINT YOUR NAME ABOVE IN UPPER CASE

Instructions to claim your free eBook edition:
1. Download the Shelfie app for Android or iOS
2. Write your name in **UPPER CASE** above
3. Use the Shelfie app to submit a photo
4. Download your eBook to any device

with...

In an effort to support local communities, raise awareness and funds, Morgan James Publishing donates a percentage of all book sales for the life of each book to

Habitat for Humanity Peninsula and Greater Williamsburg.

Get involved today! Visit
www.MorganJamesBuilds.com

TABLE OF CONTENTS

FOREWORD

In 1996, having graduated from high school 20 years earlier, I realized that advancement to senior police administration would require my return to higher education. When searching for a major, I took the advice I had been giving officers under my command for years. I chose a field of study that especially intrigued me—Applied Behavioral Science—resisting the temptation to go the more expedient and natural route and select the discipline I had been working in for the previous 18 years—Criminal Justice.

As a criminal justice professional, I have always been fascinated with the causes of behavior. Why do people do what they do, and what can be done to improve their behavior? As I progressed to the position of Chief of Police, many opportunities to apply behavioral science presented itself, both in working with the public and with those colleagues I supervised, managed, and/or advised.

I was introduced to the Actively Caring for People (AC4P) Movement by Bobby Kipper, a professional I greatly respect for his forward thinking approaches to not only law enforcement, but to life in general. Kipper, a prolific author, introduced me to Performance Driven Leadership, and my agency became the first Performance Driven Organization in the country.

As Bobby explained the application of Dr. Scott Geller's AC4P principles to law enforcement and public safety, I was instantly excited. I realized that key principles I had studied while pursuing my degree in Behavioral Science were now promoted as a pathway to improve police-citizen relations throughout a community. As I explained the AC4P Policing process to my staff, my excitement became infectious. It quickly became apparent that by engaging in the process of AC4P Policing, we would be furthering basic tenants of proactive community policing.

As you discover the AC4P principles and procedures, I encourage you to expand your perspective beyond traditional law enforcement and consider ways to initiate AC4P Policing in your community. Once you experience the flexibility, practicality, and positive impact of applying AC4P principles for citizen-centered policing, you will behold limitless possibilities for cultivating large-scale beneficial change.

Brett C. Railey, Chief of Police
Winter Park Police Department,
Winter Park, FL

THE INITIATION AND EVOLUTION OF AC4P POLICING

Scott Geller[1] coined the term "actively caring" in 1990 while working with a team of safety leaders at Exxon Chemical in Baytown, Texas. His vision was to cultivate a brother/sister keeper's culture in which everyone looks out for each other's safety on a daily basis. This requires people to routinely go above and beyond the call of duty on behalf of the health, safety, and well-being of others. The team agreed "actively caring for people" was an ideal label for this company-wide paradigm shift. Most people do care about the well-being of others, but relatively few individuals "act" on behalf of such caring in the best ways. The challenge: to get everyone acting effectively on their caring—to *actively care*.

Following the VT tragedy on April 16, 2007 when an armed student took the lives of 32 students and faculty and injured 17 others, the AC4P concept took on a new focus and prominence for Dr. Geller and his students. In a time of great uncertainty and reflection, those most affected by the tragedy were not thinking about themselves, but rather were acting to help classmates, friends, and even strangers heal. This collective effort was manifested in an AC4P Movement for culture change (see www.ac4p.org), making the belongingness spirit of the Hokie community even stronger. Dr. Geller and his students envisioned spreading this

AC4P Movement beyond VT with a basic principle of behavioral science—positive reinforcement.

They took the green silicon wristbands, engraved with "Actively Caring for People," that Dr. Geller had been distributing at safety conferences for almost two decades, and added a numbering system to enable computer tracking of the AC4P process: *See, Act, Pass,* and *Share* (SAPS). The SAPS process asks individuals and groups to look for AC4P behavior (i.e., See) and reward such AC4P behavior with a green wristband (i.e., Act).

Wristband recipients are then requested to look for AC4P behavior from others and pass on the wristband (i.e., Pass). They are asked to document this exchange (including the nature of their AC4P behavior) at the AC4P website (www.ac4p.org), along with the wristband number. In this way, a positive recognition process is tracked worldwide (i.e., Share) as positive AC4P communication.

Let's consider the profound value of police officers becoming AC4P agents of cultivating cultures of interdependent compassion. We believe such a proactive AC4P approach would help shift the common perception of the police officer as "one who reacts to criminal activity with negative consequences" to the police officer as "a community servant leader who helps prevent crime with positive consequences." Now more than ever this perceptual and protocol shift is needed.

THE BIRTH AND GROWTH OF AC4P POLICING

In July of 2015, the vision of AC4P becoming part of the fabric of policing in America became a reality when Bobby Kipper[2] and Scott Geller partnered to establish AC4P Policing. Following a 1.5 day training program, AC4P Policing was piloted in six U.S. cities: Winter Park, FL., Prescott, AZ., Flagstaff, AZ., Coolidge, AZ., Richton Park, IL., and Norfolk, VA. In each of these communities, police officers are now establishing an AC4P Movement of community caring by recognizing the acts of citizens' kindness and awarding citizens with positive consequences, particularly an AC4P wristband. This is a dramatic change from traditional policing in which officers focus on catching unlawful behavior and following such behavior with a negative consequence.

AC4P Policing applies principles of behavioral science in an effort to promote positive police-citizen interactions. Police officers record their positive interactions with citizens at a designated website (http://www.ac4ppolicing. org/), and ongoing progress is reported in a monthly newsletter disseminated by the National Center for the Prevention of Community Violence (NCPCV). The result: Traditional reactive community policing is evolving to prevention-focused citizen-centered policing.

AC4P Policing has been heralded as an innovative model of community policing that focuses on positive officer/citizen relations, and has been promoted recently through the national media, national conference presentations, and police journals. For example, the AC4P Policing process was featured as a "Great Idea" in the September 2015 edition of *Police Chief Magazine*[3] and reviewed by Fox News (https://vimeo.com/143278806).

Following the pilot applications, AC4P Policing is growing with several additional police departments joining the Movement. In January 2016, the Florida Police Chiefs Association formally endorsed AC4P Policing. This growth has led to the development of a new national training model that features this education/training manual.[3]

This manual connects research-based principles of applied behavioral science with community policing in order to initiate and sustain citizen-centered policing. As law enforcement officers become agents of positive change by promoting and supporting AC4P behavior, they will help define and promote positive and proactive community policing in America.

THE NEED FOR AC4P POLICING

The division between reactive-punitive and proactive-relational policing is the cause of much controversy facing law enforcement today. There's no doubt law enforcement could have a greater impact through proactive relationship-building than the typical reactionary measures. The need to institutionalize a change in thinking, attitude, and behavior is obvious. How can we make this happen?

First, we must move beyond *programs* and adopt a *process* mindset. Programs end, but a process continues, evolves, and successively improves. We must move beyond slogans and acronyms, and anchor a process on evidence-based principles and procedures that enable officers to trust they are making a positive and sustainable difference. This process is *AC4P Policing.*

As explained above, AC4P stands for "Actively Caring for People." This process has been researched, implemented and found effective in various settings across our country and the world, from industry to educational and community settings.[4] We now see special value in incorporating this research-based process in community policing.

During the last decade a great deal of research and discussion have led police organizations to embrace the concept—*community policing.* However, this manual was designed to help police officers of all ranks move beyond traditional community policing to applying an evidence-based process to initiate and sustain positive citizen-centered policing. This education/training manual can serve to guide effective AC4P Policing by all police officers, from the newest recruit to Command Personnel.

Question: When and how should this innovative approach to community policing be introduced to law enforcement agencies? Currently, new officers receive education and training on such subjects as Laws of Arrest, Use of Force, Aggressive Driving, State and Local Laws, Defensive Tactics, Interview and Interrogation Procedures, as well as other topics that support a reactive mindset to policing, thereby positioning the officers to enforce laws with threats and negative consequences, as exemplified by the nationwide slogan—"Click It or Ticket".

Since many police academies and department field-training programs embrace this standard of education and training, even the newest recruits have a reactive and negative-consequence mindset toward law enforcement. The solution: Introduce the positive behavioral science approach to crime prevention at introductory law-enforcement training and education sessions, as explained in this guide book.

Indeed, the application of behavioral science to prevent undesired behavior and enhance the effectiveness of community-service agents was specified in a White House Executive Order issued in September 2015 (https://www.whitehouse.gov/the-press-office/2015/09/15/executive-order-using-behavioral-science-insights-better-serve-american). This training manual adheres to this Executive Order by illustrating a positive and preventive approach to citizen-centered community policing, from research-based principles to practical and cost-effective intervention techniques. We call this community-policing and citizen-centered approach: AC4P Policing.

AC4P Policing is founded on applied behavioral science (ABS) and involves a paradigm shift regarding the role and impact of "consequences." With AC4P Policing, consequences are used to increase the quantity and improve the quality of desired behavior. Police officers are *educated* about the rationale behind using more positive than negative consequences to manage behavior, and then they are *trained* on how to deliver positive consequences in ways that help to cultivate interpersonal trust and AC4P behavior among police officers and the citizens they serve. Such is the purpose of this education/training manual and the interactive teaching/learning process we hope will accompany our explanations of evidence-based principles and procedures.

We are honored to provide you with this first edition of our AC4P Policing Manual. We dedicate this manual to all who have chosen to serve our communities and claim the honorable title of "Police Officer". We hope you find the time, interest, and passion to answer the questions and conduct the exercises offered throughout this manual, thereby putting your new knowledge of applied behavioral science and AC4P into beneficial action. Please document your experiences with AC4P Policing and this manual, and email us feedback about how to improve the next edition.

E. Scott Geller: esgeller@vt.edu

Bobby Kipper: bobbykipper@solveviolence.com

FROM PRINCIPLES TO APPLICATIONS

This teaching/learning process is founded on seven research-based lessons or guidelines from psychology—the science of human experience. The first three lessons reflect the critical behavior-management fundamentals of positive reinforcement, observational learning, and behavior-based feedback. The subsequent four lessons are derived from humanism, but behaviorism or applied behavioral science (ABS) is essential for bringing these humanistic principles to life. The result: *humanistic behaviorism* to enhance long-term positive relations between police officers and the citizens they serve, thereby preventing interpersonal conflict, violence, and harm.[5]

Furthermore, optimal training of these seven AC4P Policing lessons calls for relevant role playing and behavioral feedback. In fact, the term "training" implies that certain information is actually practiced by the learning participants, followed by improvement-focused behavioral instruction. Without an action and feedback component, a teaching/learning session can only be considered "education" or awareness.

This manual provides both education and training. Therefore, the explanation of each research-based principle for AC4P Policing is followed by questions or scenarios to facilitate group discussion. Plus, behavioral exercises are given to practice each principle and receive supportive and corrective feedback. The sharing of opinions and ideas will illustrate the variety of relevant applications from one research-based principle.

Some of these group discussions will become brainstorming sessions of innovative applications for AC4P Policing. And, when some of these possibilities are practiced through interpersonal role playing with feedback, you will have genuine "training" that increases the probability of beneficial application in the community.

EMPLOY MORE
POSITIVE CONSEQUENCES

irst, realize that behavior is motivated by consequences. As Dale Carnegie, author of the seminal book: How *to Win Friends and Influence People*, said in 1936, "Every act you have ever performed since the day you were born was performed because you wanted something."[6] We do what we do because of the consequences we expect to get, or escape, or avoid by doing it.

Your own experience or common sense informs you of this fundamental principle from behavioral science. Question: Would you rather be influenced by positive consequences or negative consequences? Your personal experience and common sense provide the answer to this question, and it's verified by over 60 years of behavioral research.

What is your reaction to the illustration on the next page?

Does the scenario seem silly, inappropriate, or ill-advised? Could you imagine a police officer actually giving a motorist a reduced fine for speeding if s/he is buckled up? What might be a driver's reaction to receiving such a positive consequence in this situation?

In what ways could this simple and practical addition to the enforcement of compliance to speed limits influence the attitudes and behaviors of vehicle drivers and occupants?

The most efficient and effective way to improve both behavior and attitude at the same time is to follow desirable behavior with a positive consequence. In fact, what happens to one's attitude when undesirable behavior is followed by a negative consequence? We all know the answer to this rhetorical question, right? But if we realize the attitudinal and behavioral advantages of using positive rather than negative consequences to influence behavior, *why are negative consequences used more often than positive consequences to improve behavior at home, in organizations, and throughout communities?*

Please record your answers to this question here and then participate in a group discussion about answers, if possible.

_____

_____

_____

_____

A MATTER OF MINDSET

Note how the answers reflect this very principle: Behavior change techniques that are most convenient and rewarded with immediate impact are most popular, at least over the short term. But discuss answers to this question: *Which behavior-change technique will have the longest-term beneficial impact? Why?*

_____

_____

_____

_____

_____

_____

_____

Often, the same situation can be viewed as: a) control by penalizing unwanted behavior, or b) control by rewarding desired behavior. Some students in Professor Geller's university classes, for example, are motivated to avoid failure (i.e., a poor grade); while other students are motivated to achieve success (e.g., a good grade or increased knowledge).

Which students feel more empowered and in control of their class grade? Which ones have a better attitude toward the class? Of course, you know the answers. Reflect on your own feelings or attitude in similar situations where you perceived your behavior was influenced by either positive or negative consequences.

Figure 1 on the next page depicts four distinct achievement-related states that have been researched by behavioral scientists to explain differences in people's attitude and motivation when working to achieve success versus avoid failure.

It's most desirable to be a *success seeker*. These are the optimists who respond to setbacks in a positive and adaptive manner. They are self-confident and willing to accept challenges, as opposed to evading demanding tasks to avoid failure.

*Figure 1. Motivational typologies defined
by achieving success vs. avoiding failure*

They wake up each day to an *opportunity* clock rather than an *alarm* clock. It's a mindset or attitude toward life you can influence in yourself and others with situational manipulations and communication, both interpersonal and intrapersonal (i.e., self-talk).

Failure avoiders have a low expectancy for success and a high fear of failure. They do whatever it takes to protect themselves from appearing incompetent. They often set low expectations and use defensive pessimism to shield themselves from experiencing failure. These individuals are motivated but are not "happy campers". They are the students who say, "I've *got* to go to class; it's a *requirement*," rather than, "I *get* to go to class; it's an *opportunity*".

Discussion Question: What kinds of conversations do you have with others and to yourself that influence a success-seeking over a failure-avoiding mindset, and vice versa?

Bottom line: Applying soon, certain and positive consequences is the most effective way to improve behavior and attitude at the same time. Using this life lesson on a daily basis is both critical and challenging. Why? Because we seem to live in a "click-it-or-ticket" culture that relies on negative consequences to manage behavior, from the classroom and workplace to our homes, and during our travel in between. Indeed, the government approach to behavior management is to pass a law and enforce it. Who are the visible enforcement agents of our society?

Discussion Questions: Given the law-enforcement responsibility of police officers, what attitudes and emotions are typically associated with police officers?

_____

_____

_____

_____

_____

_____

_____

_____

Share experiences of perceived positive and negative attitudes or emotions connected to the police officer's uniform and vehicle. What kinds of positive consequences could turn this around?

_____

_____

_____

_____

_____

_____

_____

_____

BENEFIT FROM OBSERVATIONAL LEARNING.

I f you want to be better at what you do, watch someone who performs that behavior better than you. Of course, we all realize the power of observational learning. Indeed, a large body of psychological research indicates this type of learning is involved to some degree in almost everything we do.[7]

Our actions influence others to a greater extent than we realize. Children learn by watching us at home, and our colleagues are influenced by our actions at work. We're often unaware of such influence. Consider what children learn by watching the driving behavior of their parents, including their parent's verbal behavior.

As depicted in the illustration on the next page, most parents don't realize the dramatic influence of their behavior on their children's actions. The poem below illustrates the power of observational learning.

The eye's a better teacher and more willing than the ear;
Fine counsel is confusing, but example's always clear;
And the best of all the preachers are the ones who live their creeds.
For to see the good in action is what everybody needs.

I can soon learn how to do it if you'll let me see it done;
I can watch your hands in action,
but your tongue too fast may run;
And the lectures you deliver may be very wise and true.
But I'd rather get my lesson by watching what you do.
For I may not understand you and the high advice you give.
There's no misunderstanding how you act and how you live.
—Forrest H. Kirkpatrick

THE PUBLIC VIEW OF POLICE

Consider how people's attitudes about police officers are influenced by their observation of only one interaction between a police officer and another person. Given the critical reactive dimension of their job, law-enforcement officers are typically involved in negative confrontations with citizens, often resulting in the apprehension of one or more persons. Unfortunately, this is the aspect of many situations involving police officers that is most likely to be displayed by the news media.

There are many more positive than negative interactions between police officers and citizens, right? It's just that most of these positive exchanges between police and the people they serve are never publicized. Unless, of course, police officers are responding to a newsworthy emergency and helping those needing assistance. However, a large proportion of the crises reported in the news involve experts from the other helping professions, from fire fighters to healthcare workers.

What is the visible role of the police officer in large-scale emergencies or threats to security? Crowd control or chasing suspects or perpetrators, right? Of course, these protective behaviors are terribly important, but they do not define a "police officer" right? Unfortunately, these images do define the general public perception of the police officer, derived from their observational learning.

The daily behaviors of police officers are actually more proactive than reactive, and involve more positive than negative interactions with citizens, right? However, most citizens do not see these positive proactive interactions with police officers, and therefore they don't learn about the positive side of policing.

A NEED FOR DISCUSSION

Many statements in the previous section ended with "right?" While this addition turned each statement into a rhetorical question—one that implied a "yes" response—it would be useful and educational to discuss reasons for the "yes" answer to these rhetorical questions. In other words, what personal experiences justify a "yes" answer?

Let's start at the top, and entertain a rationale for the "yes" answer from personal observational learning. If you are studying this guidebook alone, we suggest you write your answers in the space provided.

1. Are experiences between police officers and citizens more frequently positive than negative? Please justify your answer, which we hope is "yes," with examples from your personal experience and/or from your observational learning.

_____

_____

_____

_____

_____

_____

_____

_____

2. How many, if any, of the *positive* exchanges between one or more police officers and one or more citizens were reported in the news? How could more people learn about these positive interactions, especially through observational learning?

_____

_____

_____

_____

_____

_____

_____

3. List some of the proactive roles expected of police officers, but not typically covered by the news media and thus not viewed by the public.

_____

_____

_____

_____

_____

_____

4. To what extent did observational learning influence your decision to become a police officer? In other words, what observed behaviors of police officers, if any, inspired you to become a law-enforcement official?

_____

_____

_____

_____

_____

_____

5. What particular policing behaviors have you learned by watching other police officers? Please explain.

_____

_____

_____

_____

_____

_____

IMPROVE WITH BEHAVIORAL FEEDFORWARD AND FEEDBACK

"**P**ractice makes perfect" is not true; practice makes permanence. Only with behavior-focused feedback can practice improve behavior. Sometimes feedback is a natural consequence, as when the golfer and tennis player see where their ball lands after swinging a golf club or tennis racket. But even when we observe the outcome of our behavior, behavioral feedback from an observer (e.g., a coach) is necessary for proper behavioral adjustment and improvement.

People want to be competent at tasks they believe are meaningful or worthwhile. Effective policing to keep citizens safe and secure is certainly worthwhile work. So how can a police officer become more competent or effective?

You know the answer: relevant behavior-focused feedback. But who should deliver such improvement feedback? Another obvious answer: Police officers need to give each other supportive and corrective feedback.

The letters of COACH say it all: "C" for Care; "O" for Observe; "A" for Analyze; "C" for Communicate, and "H" for Help, as depicted in Figure 2 on the next page.

The coaching process starts with caring. "Know I *Care* and you'll care what I know. I care so much, I'm willing to *Observe* you and notice the occurrences of

Figure 2. The five basic components of AC4P coaching

desirable (or effective) and undesirable (or ineffective) behavior." The observer also notes environmental factors that may be influencing the observed behavior, from environmental conditions to behavioral consequences. This is the *Analysis* phase of coaching.

Next, we have interpersonal *Communication*—the delivery of information gained from the prior *Observation* and *Analysis* steps. Most people want to improve; but many people resist giving and receiving the kind of communication critical to beneficial behavior change.

Some people perceive feedback that implies personal change as an indictment of their current work style, job skills, or diligence. This reaction is most likely to happen when someone is being asked to change dramatically, and when current procedures have been followed for years.

To overcome resistance to behavioral feedback, effective behavior-improvement coaches steer clear of disruptive and dramatic communication and emphasize incremental fine tuning or successive approximations. They also facilitate beneficial change to both behavior and attitude by accentuating the positives—the occurrences of desirable behavior.

If the interpersonal communication goes well, the last letter of COACH—*Help*—is accomplished. The behavioral feedback was accepted and will be used to improve the pinpointed behavior. Note how the four letters of HELP—Humor, Esteem, Listen, and Praise—reflect strategies to increase the probability that a coach's advice, directions, or feedback will be appreciated.

MISUSE OF FEEDBACK

Imagine you receive an email from the "Chief" requesting that you come to his office at the end of the day to receive some "feedback". How would you feel? Would you anticipate a "feedback session" with unpleasant verbal behavior and emotion? How relevant is the illustration below?

Two common characteristics of feedback influence people's desire to avoid feedback, and justify the negative attitude or emotion. First, negative or *corrective* feedback is typically given more often than positive or *supportive* feedback. Many police officers have experienced this issue within their own agencies.

In other words, most parents, teachers, coaches, supervisors, and police officers use reprimands more often than praise, with the apparent belief we learn more from our mistakes than our successes. Empirical research and even common sense indicate this is untrue.

The second reason feedback has a negative connotation is that people often correct others without focusing entirely on their behavior. In other words, the feedback delivery suggests the problem or error observed reflects more than behavior. The child is "sloppy"; the student is "ignorant"; the athlete is "lazy"; the perpetrator is inherently "evil"; or the worker is "careless". That kind of feedback delivery can do more harm than good, and substantial research demonstrates dramatic disadvantages of labeling people beyond their behavior and effort even when the label is positive.[8]

It's easier said than done, but it's essential to separate behavior from person factors when giving and receiving feedback. Corrective feedback is not an indictment of one's personality or an indicator of a character flaw. Feedback must not be related to an individual's attitude, motivation, professional competence, or family history. Feedback is only about observed behavior.

Yes, responding well to supportive or corrective feedback can lead to improvement in attitude, motivation, competence, and even a personality state. But the purpose of feedback is only to pinpoint desired and/or undesired behavior. When this is realized by those who give and receive feedback, the beneficial outcome of behavioral coaching is maximized. There's room for improvement in most everything we do, and only by receiving and accepting behavior-based feedback can we do better.

IT'S IN THE DELIVERY

We hope it's clear that giving interpersonal feedback at the right time can certainly increase its beneficial impact on behavior. Actually, timing is one of four basic guidelines we recommend you consider when planning feedback strategies. These rules of feedback delivery can be readily remembered with the key words—*Specific, On time, Appropriate, and Real*—whose first letters spell "soar." So, by following these four basic rules of feedback delivery, you can "soar" to success with interpersonal feedback.

Specific. As indicated above, feedback needs to focus on specific behavior. As a *consequence* (for motivation), feedback specifies what behavior to stop and what behavior to keep performing. And as an *activator* (or directive), feedback reminds an individual to perform a particular task in a certain way. Such feedback needs to be given with straightforward and objective words, and is actually *feedforward*.

Figure 3 below illustrates the activator-behavior-consequence (ABC) model of ABS. Note the distinction between feedforward and feedback depicted in this figure. Both of these behavior-improvement techniques need to be understood and accepted by the relevant person(s). People can obviously misperceive, misunderstand, or deny the feedforward or feedback.

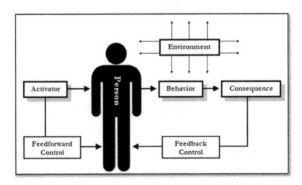

Figure 3: The ABC Model of ABS that distinguishes Feedforward from Feedback

Thus, the principles covered here suggest ways to ensure the acceptance and appreciation of behavioral direction (feedforward) and behavioral support or correction (feedback).

Ambiguous and subjective language about internal person states are not useful, and can be counterproductive. For example, evaluative statements like, "It seems you're careless, lazy, unenthusiastic, unaware, disorganized, or out-of-touch" will only add resentment and lessen the acceptability of the behavioral message. And, when you give positive statements watch for the use of "but".

Rather than giving pure praise or appreciation, we often feel obligated to add a negative statement to balance the communication. "I like the way you clarified concepts with real-world and relevant examples, *but* next time try to facilitate more involvement from your audience." Such mixed messages can weaken your impact. Some people will hear only the negative and miss the positive. Others will discount both messages, figuring the net gain of one positive and one negative is no communication.

So it's often best to make your specific behavior-focused feedback "short and sweet". Rather than combining both positive and negative feedback in one exchange or overloading a person with several behaviors to continue or change, focus your advice on one area of performance. It's much better to give people brief and specific feedback messages over weeks or months, than to give people fewer but longer feedback sessions with mixed and potentially confusing motives and directives.

On Time. As discussed above, motivational feedback to increase or decrease the occurrence of behavior should follow the target behavior as soon as possible. On the other hand, when the purpose of behavioral feedback is to shape the quality of a response, it usually makes most sense to give such directive feedback as an activator (i.e., feedforward) that precedes the next opportunity to perform the target behavior.

Receiving feedback about an error as a consequence can be perceived as punishing and frustrating, if an opportunity to correct the observed error is not available in the near future. When the person eventually receives an opportunity to correct the behavior, the advice might be forgotten. By providing advice to improve as close as possible to the next opportunity for the behavior to reoccur (i.e., as feedforward), you are increasing its directive influence and reducing the potential of a negative attitude resulting from catching a person making a mistake.

Appropriate. Specific and well-timed feedforward and feedback need to be appropriate for the needs, abilities, and expectations of the person receiving direction, support, or correction. Simply put, the feedforward and feedback should fit the situation. This means feedforward and feedback should be expressed in language the performer can understand and appreciate, and it should be customized for the performer's abilities at the particular task.

When people are learning a task, directive feedforward and motivational feedback need to be detailed and perhaps accompanied with a behavioral demonstration. In such learning situations (i.e., observational learning), it's important to match the advice with the performer's achievement level. Don't expect too much, and thus give more advice than the individual can grasp in one feedforward exchange.

At times, sub-par behavior is performed by experienced police officers who know how to do the job well, but they may have developed sub-optimal habits or are just taking a short-cut for efficiency. It could be insulting and demeaning to give these individuals detailed instructions about the appropriate way to complete their job. In these situations, it's best to give feedforward as a reminder to take the extra time for effectiveness over efficiency. Preceding your reminder with the words, "As you know," could increase acceptance of the reminder.

Consequently, it's important for the behavioral coach to size up the situation, and make specific and timely feedforward or feedback fit the occasion. This is not easy, and requires up-to-date awareness of the performer's knowledge and abilities with regard to a certain task. It also requires specific knowledge regarding the optimal ways to perform the task in a given situation. This is a prime reason why the most effective coaching usually occurs between police officers on the same team, or at least from the same department.

Real. Another reason interpersonal coaching is most effective when occurring between team members: Such feedback is often perceived as most genuine and caring. Feedforward and feedback will be ineffective if the verbal behavior is viewed as a way of exerting top-down control, or demonstrating superior knowledge, competence, or motivation. The only reason for giving behavioral feedforward or feedback is to improve and maintain the competence of team members.

Although well-intentioned, the discipline policies in some organizations make it difficult for some people to view corrective feedback as caring and supporting. The "gotcha" mindset associated with "law enforcement" can interfere with a police chief's sincere attempt to correct sub-optimal behavior. Thus, corrective feedback is most likely to be perceived as genuine or "real" when it occurs between police officers on the same team. These individuals know most about the situation and the person, and thus have sufficient information and opportunity to make the feedforward and feedback specific, on time, appropriate, and real.

IN SUMMARY

We have reviewed key guidelines for delivering effective interpersonal feedforward and feedback. In this regard the word "SOAR" is a useful teaching/learning tool, because each letter of this acronym reflects a key word that implicates a rule for delivering feedforward and feedback effectively—**S**pecific, **O**n time, **A**ppropriate, and **R**eal.

These four words indicate the special value of team members giving each other on-the-job feedforward and feedback. Why, because team members have the most complete knowledge of the feedforward/feedback recipient and the situation. Therefore, they are best able to make their behavioral feedforward and feedback: a) *specific* in terms of behavior to initiate, continue or stop, b) *appropriate* for the knowledge, abilities, and experiences of the performer, and c) reflect *real* concern for the individual's competence and job effectiveness.

Members of a work team are also most likely to be *on time* with feedforward or feedback, whether the communication serves as an activator, motivator, or both. When using feedback to support desirable behavior or decrease undesirable behavior, "on time" means the feedback should be delivered as a consequence that follows as soon after the observed behavior as possible.

In contrast, when using feedforward to encourage behavior (perhaps as a correction for sub-par behavior observed earlier), you should consider this communication a reminder or an activator. That is, you should wait for a situation that calls for the particular behavior and then offer a specific, appropriate, and genuine reminder. Thus, the right interpersonal feedforward or feedback will enable you to "soar" to new heights of policing effectiveness.

Discussion Questions

It would be extremely useful to discuss these four guidelines for giving feedforward and feedback in situations and under circumstances relevant for the participants. The format for connecting the principles with realistic applications can vary markedly. The instructor could facilitate commentary from all participants. Or, the participants could be divided into small groups; and after the questions and issues posed here are discussed, a representative from each group should report their perspectives to the entire group of participants.

Whatever your protocol for encouraging interactive discussion of feedforward and feedback, we suggest consideration of the following questions. In some teaching/learning situations it might be optimal or most convenient for participants to write personal reactions to these questions before a discussion with one or more other participants.

1. What specific situations could be benefitted with interpersonal feedforward and feedback between police officers? Is such communication more important or appropriate under some circumstances than others? Please explain.

_____

_____

_____

_____

_____

_____

2. What factors hold police officers back from giving each other behavior-based feedforward or feedback?

_____

_____

_____

_____

_____

_____

3. How might the barriers to giving each other behavior-improvement feedforward or feedback be overcome?

_____

_____

_____

_____

_____

_____

4. Please discuss personal experiences in which you *received* behavior-based feedforward and feedback from a colleague. How were these communication exchanges appropriate or inappropriate with regard to the SOAR guidelines?

_____

_____

_____

_____

_____

_____

5. Please discuss personal experiences in which you *delivered* another person behavior-focused feedforward and feedback. How were these communications appropriate or inappropriate with regard to the SOAR guidelines?

_____

_____

_____

_____

_____

_____

6. Please discuss situations when you give citizens feedforward and feedback as part of your job.

_____

_____

_____

_____

_____

7. How could your typical feedforward and feedback communications with the public be improved with application of the SOAR guidelines?

_____

_____

_____

_____

_____

_____

_____

_____

_____

_____

8. What holds you back from having more effective feedforward and feedback conversations with the citizens you serve?

_____

_____

_____

_____

_____

_____

_____

_____

_____

_____

USE MORE SUPPORTIVE
THAN CORRECTIVE FEEDBACK

"We can't learn unless we make mistakes." How many times have you heard this? While this might make us feel better about the errors of our ways, and provide an excuse for focusing more on other people's failures than on their successes, nothing could be further from the truth. Behavioral scientists have shown convincingly that success—not failure—produces the most effective learning.[9]

Edward Lee Thorndike, for example, studied intelligence at the start of the last century by putting chickens, cats, dogs, fish, monkeys, and humans in situations that called for problem-solving behavior. Then he systematically observed how these organisms learned. He coined the "Law of Effect" to refer to the fact that learning depends upon behavioral consequences.[10] And, markedly more learning occurred following positive consequences (success) than negative consequences (failure).

Does an error have to occur in order to solve a problem? We can reflect on our own experiences to answer this question. A pleasant consequence gives us direction and motivation to continue the behavior. We know what we did to receive the reward, and are thus motivated to earn another.

23

In contrast, a negative consequence following a mistake only tells us what not to do. It provides no specific direction for problem solving. An overemphasis on a mistake can be frustrating and discouraging, and actually de-motivate us to continue the learning process.

Errors are not necessary for learning to occur. In fact, when training results in no errors, made possible with certain presentation techniques, learning occurs most smoothly and is most enjoyable.[9] Errors disrupt the teaching/learning process and can lead to a negative attitude, especially if negative social consequences accentuate the mistake. Even subtle reactions to an error—a disappointed face or verbal tone—can increase feelings of helplessness or despair and turn a person off to the entire learning process.

The most powerful positive consequence to support a learning process is supportive feedback—the theme of this discussion. But, some attempts to be positive and supportive are ineffective, as the illustration below shows. Five basic guidelines are given next for giving quality supportive feedback.

BE TIMELY

In order for supportive feedback to provide optimal direction and support, it needs to be associated directly with the desired behavior, as *not* demonstrated in the illustration. When people know what they did to earn the appreciation, they might be motivated to continue that behavior.

If it's necessary to delay the supportive feedback, the conversation should relive the activity deserving recognition. Talk specifically about the behavior that warrants special acknowledgement. Don't hesitate to ask the recipient to recall aspects of the situation and the commendable behavior. This enables direction and motivation to continue the desired behavior.

MAKE IT PERSONAL

Supportive feedback is most meaningful when it's perceived as personal. Verbal support should not be generic, fit for any situation, as in "Nice job". Rather, it needs to be customized to fit a particular individual and circumstance. This happens naturally when the supportive feedback is linked to designated behavior. When you recognize someone, you're expressing personal thanks.

Sometimes it's tempting to say "*we* appreciate" rather than "*I* appreciate," and to refer to departmental gratitude rather than *personal appreciation*. But, speaking for an organization or company can come across as impersonal and insincere.

Of course, it's appropriate to reflect value to the organization when giving supportive feedback, but the focus should be personal: "I saw what you did to support our AC4P Policing process and I really appreciate it. "*Your example demonstrates the kind of leadership we need around here to improve police-community relations.*" This second statement illustrates the next guideline for giving quality supportive feedback.

TAKE IT TO A HIGHER LEVEL

Supportive feedback is most memorable and inspirational when it reflects a higher-order quality. Adding a universal attitude like leadership, integrity, or trustworthiness, or AC4P to your recognition statement makes the feedback more meaningful and thus rewarding. It's important to state the specific behavior first, and then make an obvious linkage between the behavior and the positive character trait it reflects.

Later, we discuss the use of an AC4P wristband to show appreciation for AC4P-related behavior. In these cases, we offer the wristband as a symbol of AC4P leadership and worn to show membership in an elite group of individuals dedicated to cultivating an AC4P culture of compassion. Thus, the AC4P wristband is given to not only reward AC4P behavior, but also to signify membership in a Movement to cultivate AC4P cultures of interpersonal compassion.

This connection brings the interpersonal supportive feedback to a higher level, enabling positive impact on the recipient's self-esteem, competence, and sense of interdependence and belongingness. Later we explain how these person-states enhance self-motivation and the propensity to perform more AC4P behavior.

DELIVER IT PRIVATELY

Because supportive feedback is personal and indicative of higher-order attributes, it needs to be delivered privately and one-on-one. This requires a certain degree of courage for those not comfortable in private, one-on-one conversations; especially with people they don't know well. But consider this: The verbal support is special and only relevant to one person. So, it will mean more and seem more genuine if it's given personally—from one individual to another.

It seems conventional to recognize individuals in front of a group. This approach is typified in athletic contests and reflected in the pop-psychology slogan, "Praise publicly and reprimand privately". Many managers take the lead from this common-sense statement and give individuals recognition in group settings.

Indeed, isn't it maximally rewarding to be held up as an exemplar in front of one's peers? Not necessarily, because many people feel embarrassed when singled out in front of a group. Part of this embarrassment could be due to fear of subsequent harassment by peers. Some peers might call the recognized individual an "apple-polisher" or "brown-noser," or accuse him or her of "sucking up to management".

In athletic events the participants' performance is measured objectively and therefore winners are determined fairly. However in educational and work settings it's usually impossible to assess everyone's relevant behaviors objectively and obtain a fair ranking for individual recognition. Hence, praising one individual in public may lead to perceptions of inequality or favoritism from individuals who feel they did equally well, but did not get praised. Plus, such ranking sets up a win-lose atmosphere—perhaps appropriate for some sporting events—but not in settings where interdependent teamwork is needed to achieve group goals.

LET IT SINK IN

In this fast-paced age of trying to do more with less, we try to communicate as much as possible when we finally get in touch with a busy person. After recognizing an individual's special AC4P effort, we are tempted to tag on a bunch of unrelated statements, even a request for additional behavior. This comes across as, "I appreciate what you've done, but I need more".

Resist the temptation to do more than praise the AC4P behavior you saw. If you have additional points to discuss, it's best to reconnect later, after the supportive feedback has had a chance to sink in and become part of the individual's self-talk for self-recognition and self-motivation.

By giving supportive recognition, we give people a script they can use to reward their own behavior. In other words, supportive feedback strengthens the other person's self-reward system. And, positive self-talk (or self-recognition) is critical for long-term maintenance of desired behavior. Thus, by allowing supportive feedback to stand alone and sink in, we enable the internalization of rewarding words that can be used later for self-motivation to perform the recognized behavior again.

ACCEPT SUPPORTIVE FEEDBACK

Most of us get so little supportive feedback from others that we are caught completely off guard when acknowledged for our commendable actions. We don't know how to accept recognition when it finally comes. Don't shy away when it does come; have the courage to embrace it. Remember the basic behavioral-science principle: Consequences influence the behaviors they follow.

As our first lesson explained, positive consequences increase the probability that the behavior recognized will continue. Plus, one's reaction to the supportive feedback influences whether the observer will attempt to provide supportive feedback again. Thus, it's crucial to react appropriately when we receive recognition from others. Let's consider seven basic guidelines for receiving supportive behavioral feedback.

Don't deny or disclaim. Often when we attempt to give supportive recognition, we get a reaction that implies we're wasting our time. We get disclaimer statements like, "It really was nothing special"; "Just doing my job". The most common reply: "No problem." This implies the behavior recognized was not special and did not warrant supportive feedback.

Supportive feedback needs to be accepted without denial or disclaimer statements, and without deflecting the credit to others. It's okay to show pride in our small-win accomplishments, even if others contributed to the successful outcome. After all, the vision of compassionate AC4P policing includes everyone going beyond the call of duty on behalf of the well-being of others. In this context, numerous people deserve recognition daily.

Accept the fact that supportive feedback will be intermittent at best for everyone. So when your turn comes, accept the feedback for your recognized behavior and for the many prior desirable behaviors you performed that went unnoticed. Keep in mind your genuine appreciation of the supportive feedback will increase the likelihood the person who gave you feedback will give more behavioral recognition to others. Plus, you might be inspired to do the same, given that you recognize personal benefit from the feedback and want others to experience such behavioral support.

Listen actively. Listen actively to the person recognizing you with supportive feedback. Certainly, you want to learn what you did right. Plus, you can evaluate whether the supportive feedback is given well. If the feedback does not pinpoint a particular behavior, you might ask the person, "What did I do to deserve this?" This will help to improve that person's method of giving supportive feedback.

Of course, it's important to show genuine appreciation for the special attention. Consider how difficult it is for many people to go out of their way to recognize others with supportive feedback. So, revel in the fact that you're receiving some behavioral recognition, even if its quality could be improved.

Use it later for self-motivation. Most of your competent behaviors go unnoticed. You perform many of these behaviors when no one else is around to observe you. Even when other people are available, they are usually so preoccupied with their own routines they don't notice your extra effort. So when you finally do receive supportive feedback, take it in as well-deserved.

Don't hesitate to relive this moment later by talking to yourself. Such self-recognition can motivate you to continue going beyond the call of duty as an AC4P police officer. As mentioned earlier, self-talk can help you muster the self-motivation to perform more of the recognized behavior.

Show sincere appreciation. You need to show sincere gratitude with a smile, a "Thank You," and perhaps special words like, "You've made my day." Your reaction to receiving supportive feedback can determine whether similar recognition will be delivered by that person again. So be prepared to offer a sincere "Thank You," and words that reflect your pleasure in the memorable positive interaction. And consider the courage the other person might have needed to give you that personal recognition.

We find it natural to add, "You've made my day" to the "Thank-You" because it's the truth. When people go out of their way to offer us quality recognition, they *have* made our day. In fact, we often relive such situations to improve a later day.

Reward the recognizer. When you accept supportive feedback well, you reward the person for his or her appreciating behavior. This can motivate that individual to deliver more positive feedback, especially if the person is more of an introvert and requires courage to step out and speak up to give recognition.

Sometimes, you can even do more to assure the occurrence of more supportive feedback. Specifically, you can recognize the person for recognizing you. You might say, for example, "I really appreciate you noticing my behavior and calling me a leader of the AC4P policing process." Such supportive and rewarding feedback provides direction and motivation for those aspects of AC4P policing that are especially worthwhile and need to become routine.

Ask for recognition. If you feel you deserve supportive feedback, why not ask for it? You will likely view this recognition as less genuine than if it were spontaneous, but the outcome from such a request can be quite beneficial. You might receive some words worth reliving later for self-motivation. Most importantly, you will remind the other individual in a nice way that s/he missed a prime opportunity to offer supportive feedback. This could be a valuable learning experience for that person.

Consider the possible beneficial impact from your statement to another person that you are pleased with a certain outcome of your extra effort. With the right tone and affect, such verbal behavior will not seem like bragging but rather a declaration of personal pride in a small-win accomplishment—something more people should feel and relive for self-motivation. The other person will surely support your personal praise with supportive testimony, and this will bolster your self-motivation. Plus, you will teach the other person how to support the commendable behavior of others.

THE CRAVING

William James, the first renowned American psychologist wrote, "The deepest principle in human nature is the craving to be appreciated".[11] Then in 1936, Dale Carnegie advocated the key to winning friends and influencing people is to "always make the other person feel important".[11] How can we readily fulfill the human need to feel appreciated and important? The answer, of course: Give and receive supportive feedback.

FROM PRINCIPLES TO PRACTICE

Before applying the interpersonal feedback techniques we discussed here in the field, we suggest participants role-play the procedures for delivering supportive and corrective feedback. Such role-play should be followed with systematic behavioral feedback from the instructor (and other participants). The delivery of this feedback should follow the guidelines presented here, thereby providing observational learning for the participants. In addition, we recommend the participants practice the recommended feedback techniques on family members before taking their behavior-improvement techniques to the "street".

Also, we suggest the participants work on mastering supportive feedback before attempting corrective feedback. Supportive feedback, or behavioral recognition, is much easier to employ than corrective feedback, and can do no harm if applied incorrectly. On the other hand, inappropriate application of corrective feedback could result in a negative attitude or hurt feelings from the recipient that could interfere with future interactions between these colleagues.

After discussing the benefits of providing supportive and corrective feedback, the instructor should review the basic delivery and receiving steps for effective supportive feedback, as detailed above. Then, the participants should pair off and practice giving each other supportive feedback. One participant should agree to be the feedback "sender" and the other is the "recipient". Then, a particular policing situation and behavior should be defined for the role-play exercise. This could be a real-world situation the participants have actually experienced, or only a possibility for delivering feedback.

After receiving the supportive feedback, the recipients should express their reaction to the feedback. Did the feedback seem genuine? Did the feedback address a specific behavior? Did the recipient feel rewarded by the interchange? Afterwards, the roles should be reversed, with the "sender" playing the role of "recipient" and vice versa.

The instructor/facilitator should circulate among the practicing role-players and note examples of particularly effective and ineffective performance. These observations could then be discussed when the participants reconvene as a group. Group members should discuss their feedback experiences from the perspectives of both the "sender" and the "recipient" of supportive feedback.

Group leaders might select a feedback pair who displayed exemplary performance during the role-play sessions and ask these participants to demonstrate their interaction skills to the rest of the group. The group facilitator might offer supportive and corrective feedback to the presenters, and then ask other participants to contribute supportive and corrective feedback.

After role-playing and gaining confidence in your ability to "catch good behavior" and give genuine supportive feedback, you are ready to reap the benefits of real-world experience. Observe the ongoing behaviors of certain individuals (perhaps starting with family members). After noting a "good" behavior, apply the supportive feedback process. Document your experience by completing the chart below. After completing this chart, it would be instructive to discuss the information (especially recipient reactions) at group meetings.

Documentation of Delivering Supportive Feedback

Behavior Recognized	Environmental Setting	Reactions of Recipient
1.		
2.		
3.		
4.		
5.		
6.		

Role-playing, group demonstrations, and interactive feedback should be used to improve skills of the participants at giving *corrective feedback*. Practice sessions should follow the same basic format as that given above for *supportive* feedback, except that it will take more practice and individual direction to master this type of verbal communication.

After participants demonstrate with role-playing that they can follow the basic steps of delivering corrective feedback, they are ready to apply this new verbal skill beyond the classroom. We recommend the first few corrective feedback sessions be attempted with family members or friends, after observing an undesired (or less-than-optimal) behavior (of course).

Documentation of Real-World Corrective Feedback

Undesirable Behavior	Environmental Setting	Alternative Behavior	Recipient's Reaction
1.			
2.			
3.			
4.			

Subsequently, less-than-optimal behaviors observed among work colleagues should be the target of the corrective feedback techniques. For maximum benefit, these sessions should be documented in the chart above and discussed in group meetings among those participating in this ongoing exercise.

Finally, it would be very useful to practice and document occasions of giving feed*forward* and feed*back* to colleagues and citizens throughout your day. You should note what went well and not so well in your delivery of personal *feedback* for behavioral support or correction. Reflect on these comments as *feedforward* to improve your next opportunity to improve another person's behavior.

We hope you will use the chart below to systematically document your interpersonal feedforward and feedback experiences. Discussing these feedforward and feedback experiences among others will be instructive for all as vicarious observational learning (Lesson 3).

Documentation of Feedforward and Feedback Experiences

Feedforward or Feedback	Target Behavior	Situation or Context	Positive Outcome	Room for Improvement

Lesson 5

EMBRACE AND
PRACTICE EMPATHY

T
he rationale for using more supportive than corrective feedback to improve
behavior is based on the differential feeling states provoked by positive
versus negative consequences. Similarly, the way a behavior-improvement
process is implemented can increase or decrease feelings of empowerment, build
or destroy trust, and cultivate or inhibit a sense of teamwork or belonging.

Decisions regarding which behavior-improvement process to implement,
and how to refine existing intervention procedures should be based on both
objective observations of behaviors and subjective evaluations of feeling states.
Often, it's possible to employ *empathy* to evaluate the indirect internal impact
of an intervention. Simply imagine yourself going through a particular set of
community policing procedures. Then, ask yourself, "How would I feel?"

Empathy is not the same as sympathy, although dictionary definitions are
similar. *The New Merriam Webster Dictionary* (1989) defines sympathy as "the
capacity for entering into and sharing the feelings or interests of another" (p.
727), and empathy as "the capacity for experiencing as one's own the feelings of
another" (p. 248).

Likewise, *The American Heritage Dictionary* (1991) defines empathy as
"identification with and understanding of another's situation, feeling, and

36

motives" (p. 449), in contrast to sympathy as "a feeling or expression of pity or sorrow for the distress of another person" (p. 1231). Thus, we sympathize when we express concern or understanding for another individual's situation, but we empathize when we identify with another person's situation and realize what it's like to be in the other person's shoes.

An empathic level of awareness and appreciation is not easy to achieve, and can only be reached after we minimize the reactive filters that bias our conversations, and listen intently and proactively to another person. Not only must we hear every word, but we must also look for feelings, passion, and commitment reflected as much in body language and manner of expression as in the words themselves.

When we observe another person's behavior, we should try and view the situation from that individual's perspective. When we listen to excuses for inappropriate behavior (e.g., breaking a law), we can try and see ourselves in the same predicament. We can imagine what defense mechanisms we might use to protect our own ego or self-esteem. And when we consider action plans for improvement, we can try and view various alternatives through the eyes of the other person. As the illustration on the next page shows, those eyes of the other person are biased by personal experience.

Are you thinking it's difficult to see situations and circumstances through the eyes of another person? Are you thinking, "This is easier said than done?" Well, you're probably right. But consider that we're only talking about taking a different perspective into our conversations. We need to approach our coaching conversations with an empathic mindset.

AC4P EMPATHIC LISTENING

Sometimes, in their eagerness to make things happen, managers, coaches, teachers, parents, and police officers give feedforward directions and corrective feedback in a top-down, seemingly controlling manner. In other words, their passion to make a difference can lead to an overly directive approach to getting others to change their behavior. An indirect or nondirective approach to giving advice is usually more effective, especially over the long term, and this is a basic tenant of humanistic therapy.

Think about it: How do you respond when someone tells you exactly what to do? Now it certainly depends on who is giving the directive, but I bet your reaction is not entirely positive. You might follow the instructions, especially if it comes from someone with the power to control consequences. But how will you feel? Will you be self-motivated to make a lasting change? You might if you asked for the direction. But if you didn't request advice or feedback, you could feel insulted or embarrassed. Try to be more nondirective when using interpersonal conversation to affect behavior change. This requires empathic listening.

Dale Carnegie wrote about the value of empathic listening more than 80 years ago in his classic book: *How to Win Friends and Influence People.*[11] His wisdom is reflected in the writing of many authors of popular self-help books, including Stephen Covey's fifth habit of highly effective people, "Seek First to Understand...Then to be Understood."[12]

Carnegie, Covey, and others offer the same basic strategies for empathic listening, and if you've had any training in effective communication, you've heard the same advice. Let's review these guidelines with four easy-to-remember words, each beginning with the letter "R".

For readers who have received communication training, this review will at least provide a mnemonic for remembering how to listen with an empathic AC4P mindset and teach others to do the same. To be sure, the increasing "lean and mean" and "win/lose" paradigms of contemporary organizations, as well as the focus on impersonal emails and text messages, suggest a dire need to teach and use these humanistic guidelines for one-on-one empathic listening.

Repeat. This is the easiest technique to use. Simply mimic (or repeat) what you hear in the same words. This clarifies that you heard correctly, and most importantly, prompts the person to say more. Remember the purpose of empathic listening is to motivate the other person to say more so you can truly understand the problem.

So if a friend tells you he's dropping out of school, you might repeat this statement with, "You're dropping out?" This shows you're attentive and interested, and waiting for more information. Hearing how drastic the statement sounds, the person might reply, "Well, at least I feel like dropping out." Then, what would you say? Following this "repeat" technique, you would say, "You mean you feel like dropping out?" Or, you might use different words to echo the same meaning. This is the next empathic listening technique.

Rephrase. Instead of mimicking the content, you might rephrase the statement. In other words, say back the same thing but in different words. In our example, you might say, "You mean you don't like the life of a college student anymore?" By putting the statement in your own words, you're showing genuine interest while also asking for more information. You're also checking for understanding. If you can rephrase the statement correctly, you have received and interpreted the communication accurately.

It's possible your friend miscommunicated or you misperceived something. Your rephrasing gives the other person a chance to explain. And, this is what you want—more disclosure of the problem. Suppose your friend clarifies, "Well, it's not that I don't like being a student here, it's just that some of my teachers get me so frustrated at times, I feel like quitting."

Now, your friend has revealed a more specific strategy and you return with, "Your teachers get you frustrated." Alternatively, you could attempt to *rephrase* with something like, "You mean some of your teachers get you so angry that your motivation to continue attending classes is sapped". Or, perhaps this statement calls for the next "R" of empathic listening—*ratification.*

Ratify. With this listening strategy you demonstrate affirmations or support for the individual's statement by confirming your understanding. In other words, you offer words that show approval for what is being said, and this in turn, encourages more explanation.

In our example, you might ratify your appreciation of the statement by saying, "I know the feeling; I've been frustrated with some of my teachers at times and wonder whether this college life is for me."

At this point, you might be tempted to jump in with probing questions to find out more about the frustration, the teachers, or the situation. What teachers got you so upset? What did they do? Why are you so frustrated that you want to quit? You should resist this temptation to be directive. You probably have not heard enough about the problem to begin a structured (and unbiased) analysis.

More empathic listening could reveal problems beyond the teachers. Perhaps it's not a teacher per se, but a particular homework assignment or exam grade. Or, the problem might stem from interactions with another student, or a family member, or from feelings of personal inadequacy, including a perceived loss of confidence, self-efficacy, or personal control.

Bottom Line: A person's distress signals can come from many sources, and these will probably not come to the surface quickly in one-to-one communication. And, if the relevant causes of a problem were disclosed early, it's unlikely you could give optimal advice at this point—directive action that is both useful and accepted. Usually, the best we can do is listen actively with repeat, rephrase, and ratify strategies in order to get the problem out in the open. Ultimately, we want the person to express true feelings, as indicated by the fourth "R" word.

Reflect. When people reflect on their inner feelings about a situation, they are at the personal root of the problem. Such self-disclosure of person-states can lead to insight into the true cause of the problem (for both the speaker and the listener), and suggest strategies for intervention. However, even at this stage (with outer layers of the onion peeled away), it's usually better to let the speaker entertain a variety of possible intervention approaches.

If you've been an empathic listener, you might eventually get the ultimate reward for your sensitivity, patience, and emotional intelligence. The speaker will ask you for specific advice. When you hear words like, "What do you think I should do," you have mastered empathic listening. You have shown you actively care, and now your thoughtful direction will likely be most relevant, understood, and accepted.

ASK QUESTIONS FIRST

Suppose the conversation is not about a serious issue like personal distress, frustration, or apathy, but only about a less-than-desired behavior. You see an opportunity for a person to show more or better AC4P behavior in a particular situation. What should you say?

Instead of telling the person what to do, try this. Get the individual to tell you, in his or her own words, what s/he could have done to be more effective from an AC4P mindset. You can do this by asking questions with a sincere and empathic demeanor. Avoid at all costs a sarcastic or demeaning tone.

First, point out certain desirable behaviors you noticed—it's important to start with positives. Then move on to the less desirable behavior by asking, "Could you have been more effective in that situation?" Of course, you hope for more than a "yes" or "no" response to a question like this. But if that's all you get, you need to be more precise in follow-up questioning.

You might, for example, point out a particular situation where the behavior you observed could have been more effective, and then ask what that behavior should be. Now we're talking about giving corrective feedback, as was addressed in the prior lesson. Now you realize the value in starting corrective feedback with questions.

By asking questions, you're always going to learn something. If nothing else you'll hear the rationale behind the undesired or non-optimal behavior. You might uncover a barrier to the optimal behavior which you can help the person overcome. A conversation that entertains ways to remove obstacles that hinder desired behavior is especially valuable if it translates possibilities into feasible and relevant action plans.

Obviously, *empathic* listening, diagnosing, and action planning take patience. Conversations at this level are often not efficient, but they are always most effective. Through questioning and listening, the objective is to first learn what it's like to be in the other person's situation. Then the objective shifts to developing a corrective approach that fits the circumstances as mutually understood by everyone involved in the conversation. If commitment to follow through with a specific action plan is stated, you were an empathic behavioral coach.

FROM PRINCIPLES TO PRACTICE

Okay, we've reviewed the rationale for this empathy lesson, and we offered guidelines for accomplishing empathic listening. You've been educated. You understand the value and the purpose of empathetic listening. Can you be an effective empathic listener? Of course you can, but it may take some practice along with relevant behavioral feedback. Now we're talking about *training*. We suggest the following group exercise:

Divide the participants into pairs and ask them to find a relatively quiet location for a brief conversation. If the size of the group and/or the facility prevents private dyadic communication, simply ask participants to turn to the individual closest to them and execute this practice/feedback session on the spot. While focusing on their "private" one-to-one conversations, the participants will readily tune out the verbal noise from other dyads.

Tell the participants this exercise has two trials (if time permits). For the first trial one member of the dyad will serve as the first speaker, and the other will be the empathic listener. Then, for the second trial, the dyadic partners will switch roles. For each trial, the speaker should tell the listener a personal story, perhaps one that could benefit from another person's perspective and/or advice. Emphasize that the speakers will have a maximum of three minutes to tell their story, while the listeners practice the four R-word guidelines for empathic listening: Repeat, Rephrase, Ratify, and Reflect.

After the three-minute story, the listeners should take a maximum of two minutes to offer his/her viewpoint and advice (if relevant), while the former speaker plays the role of empathic listener. Afterwards, have each member of the dyad offer behavioral feedback regarding the demonstration of effective vs. ineffective listening skills. Start with the positives first (i.e., supportive feedback) and then offer some corrective feedback. The challenge: Practice the recommended ways of giving and receiving supportive and corrective feedback.

When considering the nature of feedback to give the listener, ask yourself these questions:

1. How did the listener facilitate continued verbal behavior from the speaker?

_____

_____

_____

_____

2. What did the listener do to enable the speaker to reveal personal aspects of his/her story?

_____

_____

_____

_____

_____

_____

_____

_____

3. Did the speaker ask for advice or did the listener offer advice without a request?

_____

_____

_____

_____

_____

_____

_____

4. Was the advice relevant and/or useful?

_____

_____

_____

_____

_____

_____

5. What particular R-word guidelines for empathic listening were used in this dyadic communication?

_____

_____

_____

_____

_____

_____

6. What could the listener have done to facilitate more revealing communication from the speaker?

_____

_____

_____

_____

_____

_____

_____

7. How did this exercise help you appreciate the value of empathic listening, and perhaps realize validity in the earlier statement, "It's not that easy"?

_____

_____

_____

_____

_____

_____

The instructor should call "Time" after the three-minute story, and also after the two-minute reaction by the listener. Then allow five minutes of feedback discussion among the dyads. Total time for Trial 1: ten minutes. If time permits, this entire exercise should be repeated with the speakers and listeners switching roles (i.e., Trial 2).

After the dyads complete one or two trials, the instructor should facilitate a group discussion about the take-a-ways from this exercise. Ask the participants to report what they learned about empathic listening from their discussions. What R-word strategies did they notice, and what were advantages, if any, of practicing these listening techniques?

_____

_____

_____

_____

_____

_____

_____

In what ways, if any, did this experience influence your intentions (i.e., feedforward) for subsequent communication with work colleagues or family members? [Note: As you know, when people make a public commitment to improve, the probability of actual improvement increases markedly.]

_____

_____

_____

_____

_____

_____

_____

DISTINGUISH BETWEEN MANAGING BEHAVIOR AND LEADING PEOPLE

M anagement is not the same as leadership. Yes, both are critically important for bringing the best out of people. Simply put, managers hold us accountable to perform desirable behavior and avoid undesirable behavior. Leaders inspire us to hold ourselves accountable to do the right thing.

Managers control behavior with an external (or extrinsic) accountability intervention or system. Leaders facilitate self-motivation by influencing person-states (e.g., perceptions, attitudes, and/or emotions) that facilitate self-motivation. Self-motivation (or self-directed behavior) often leads to *discretionary* behavior—behavior beyond that which is required.

SELF-MOTIVATION

The C-words of *Choice, Competence,* and *Community* illustrate the three evidence-based perceptions or person-states that determine self-motivation.[13] Dispositional, interpersonal, and environmental conditions that enhance these states increase personal perceptions of self-motivation. Consider, for example, how proper application of the first five lessons can increase one's perception of competence and hence fuel self-motivation. Consider, also, how our language can affect each of these perceptions.

Watch your language. Your language should suggest minimal external pressure. The common phrases: "Safety is a condition of employment," "All accidents are preventable," and "Bullying is a rite of passage," reduce one's sense of autonomy. In contrast, the slogan, "Actively caring is a core value of our organization" implies personal authenticity, interpersonal relatedness, and human interaction.

The common phrase "random acts of kindness" has a disadvantage when describing or promoting AC4P behavior. Random implies the behavior happens by chance, suggesting it's beyond individual choice or control. The kind act may appear random to the recipient, but it was likely performed intentionally and was self-motivated. An alternative: "intentional acts of kindness." The language we use to prescribe or describe behavior influences our perceptions of its meaningfulness and its relevance to our lives. Language impacts culture, and vice versa.

Opportunities for choice. Participative management means employees have personal choice during the planning, execution, and evaluation of their jobs. People have a need for autonomy, regardless of dispositional and situational factors. In the workplace, managers often tell people what to do rather than involving them in the decision-making process. Referring to language again, should managers give "mandates" or set "expectations"? Should they request "compliance" or ask for "commitment"?

In schools, students are often viewed as passive learners, because teachers plan, execute, and evaluate most aspects of the teaching/learning process. Students' perceptions of choice are limited. Yet cooperative teaching/learning, whereby students contribute to the selection and presentation of lesson material is most beneficial over the long term.

The same could be said for the role of a police officer who uncovers a specific issue within the community. A police supervisor *(or manager)* directs the officer on exactly how to handle the specific issue. In contrast, a police *leader* allows the officer opportunity to suggest and plan a course of action.

The child in the illustration below is attempting to have some choice regarding a mandate he perceives to be top-down and controlling.

Involve the followers. In police departments, autonomy or the perception of choice is supported when rules are established by soliciting input from those affected by the regulation. Police officers are more likely to comply with regulations they helped to define. Shouldn't they have substantial influence during the development of policy they will be asked to follow? Those officers on the "front line" know best what actions should be avoided versus performed in order to optimize the safety and beneficial impact of their assignments.

Similarly, before a policy or regulation is implemented in an organization, those affected (i.e., faculty, students, police officers, citizens) should certainly be given opportunities to offer suggestions. In a police department, shouldn't those officers taxed with enforcing laws and community ordinances provide input into the behavioral definitions of infractions, as well as the enforcement policies and procedures?

EMPOWERMENT

In the management literature, empowerment typically refers to delegating authority or responsibility, or to sharing decision-making. In other words, when a manager says, "I empower you," s/he usually means, "Get 'er done."

In contrast, the AC4P leader first assesses whether the "empowered" individual *feels* empowered. "Can you handle the additional assignment?" Proper assessment of feeling empowered involves asking three questions, as derived from social learning theory.

As depicted in Figure 4 below, the first question, "Can I do it?" asks whether the empowered individual or group has the resources, time, knowledge and ability to handle the assignment. The knowledge and ability components refer to training, and the term *self-efficacy* places the focus on personal belief.

An observer might think an individual has the competence to complete a task, but the empowered person might feel differently. Thus, a "yes" answer to

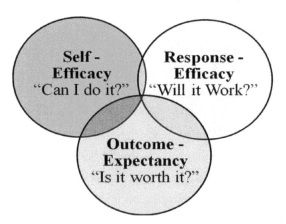

Figure 4. The three beliefs that determine empowerment

the first empowerment question implies a belief of relevant personal effectiveness by those who received the assignment or who set a performance-improvement process goal.

The second question, the response-efficacy question, asks whether those who are empowered believe pursuing and accomplishing the assignment or attaining the process goal (i.e., performing the required behaviors) will contribute to a valued mission of the organization, work team, or individual.

Regarding AC4P Policing, this translates into believing a particular proactive community policing process (e.g., whereby police officers reward certain desirable behaviors of citizens) will contribute to increasing interpersonal trust and positive relations between police and the citizens they serve, and contribute to reducing the crime rate in the community.

A sports team would answer "yes" to this question if the members believe their new workout routine or competition strategy will increase the probability of winning a game. And, the student studying for an exam would give a "yes" answer to response-efficacy if s/he believes the study strategy will contribute to earning a higher exam grade. Of course, the behavioral outcome for these two examples could be more distal and substantive, like having a winning season or obtaining a college degree, respectively.

Whereas a "no" answer to the "self-efficacy" question indicates a need for more training, education might be needed to obtain a "yes" answer to the response-efficacy question. In other words, people might believe they can accomplish a particular process or task (i.e., self-efficacy), but not believe such accomplishment will make a difference in a desired outcome (i.e., response-efficacy). In this case, education is needed, including an explanation of an evidence-based principle or theory and perhaps the presentation of convincing data.

The third empowerment-assessment question targets motivation. Is the expected outcome worth the effort? The performance of relevant behavior is motivated by anticipating a positive consequence to achieve or a negative consequence to avoid. Referring back to the first lesson, recall that people feel more choice and are more likely to be self-motivated when they perceive they are trying to achieve a positive consequence than when they are responding to avoid a negative consequence.

Empowering goals. As an activator of process activities aimed at achieving a particular outcome, behavior-focused goal setting facilitates individual and/or group success. Perhaps you are aware of a popular acronym used to define the characteristics of an effective goal: SMART. There are actually a few variations of the words reflected by these acronym letters, with *M* representing Measurable or Motivational, and *T* referring to Timely or Trackable, for example.

We propose the following acronym words: *S* for Specific, *M* for Motivational, *A* for Attainable, *R* for Relevant, and *T* for Trackable, and the addition of an *S* for Shared (i.e., SMARTS) because social support can increase commitment to work toward reaching a goal. Please note the connection between SMARTS goals and the empowerment model introduced above.

Empowerment vs. self-motivation. It's important to consider a critical distinction between these two person-states. Empowerment is a behavioral antecedent (i.e., feedforward), whereas self-motivation reflects the impact of consequences (i.e., feedback). In other words, feeling empowered means the individual is ready (or activated) to work toward achieving a given goal. On the other hand, a self-motivated person is anticipating or has received a consequence (e.g., feedback) that supports self-directed rather than other-directed behavior.

With this perspective, consequences that reflect personal choice, competence, and/or a sense of social support or community should enhance self-motivation, and thereby increase the durability of a behavior-change intervention that applies positive consequences (Lesson 1). Thus, an intervention applying positive consequences to increase the occurrence of a target behavior will have longer-term impact if the intervention inspires self-motivation by linking the behavioral consequence(s) with a perception of choice, competence, and/or community.

Figure 5 on the next page, illustrates how empowerment, vision, and goal setting fit with the ABC (activator-behavior-consequence) model discussed

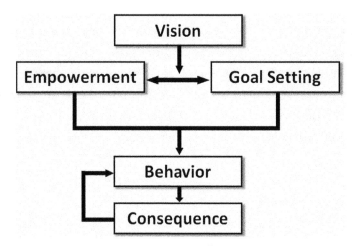

*Figure 5: The connection between goal setting,
empowerment, and consequences.*

earlier under Lesson 3. The simple but critical point: A vision and a goal are not sufficient to sustain desirable behavior. People need to feel empowered to work for goal achievement, including the acquisition of desirable consequences and/or the avoidance of undesirable consequences.

Participants need to believe in and own the vision. They need to feel encouragement from peers to attain process goals that support the vision. And peers need to give them supportive and corrective feedback to increase the quantity and improve the quality of behaviors consistent with vision-relevant goals.

Pause for a Review and Discussion
At this point, you could review the key components of this lesson (self-motivation, empowerment, and goal setting) by watching a 15-minute TEDx talk on YouTube. Simply Google Scott Geller TEDx and you can watch a spirited presentation of the basic concepts explained in this section.

Afterwards, the instructor should facilitate a discussion of answers to the following questions. Participants could write personal answers to the questions, or break up into smaller interactive groups and discuss answers among themselves before giving small-group reports to the entire group. Or, the instructor could facilitate constructive discussion of answers to the discussion questions.

Whatever format is most appropriate, the objective is to activate some interactive engagement whereby participants express their viewpoints and verbalize connections between the self-motivation concepts and their own life experiences.

Discussion Questions

1. Explain the three beliefs that determine empowerment as a psychological state, and connect each belief to ways for increasing empowerment through training, education, and motivation.

_____

_____

_____

_____

_____

_____

2. Explain the three perceptions (i.e., C-words) that influence self-motivation and provide examples from personal experience.

_____

_____

_____

_____

_____

_____

3. Explain the meaning of B. F. Skinner's legacy: "selection by consequences".

_____

_____

_____

_____

_____

_____

4. Distinguish between a "goal" and a "vision" with a personal example.

_____

_____

_____

_____

_____

_____

5. The ABC Model of behavioral science presumes behavior is *directed* by activators (or feedforward) and *motivated* by consequences (e.g., feedback). How can goal setting provide both direction and motivation?

_____

_____

_____

_____

_____

_____

_____

6. Explain the difference between independency and interdependency with regard to optimizing a work culture and bringing out the best in people.

_____

_____

_____

_____

_____

_____

7. Which of the lessons in this brief talk on self-motivation were most meaningful to you? Please explain why?

_____

_____

_____

_____

_____

_____

PROGRESS FROM SELF-ACTUALIZATION TO SELF-TRANSCENDENCE

The most popular theory of human motivation is the hierarchy of needs proposed by humanist Abraham Maslow. Categories of needs are arranged hierarchically, and it's presumed people don't attempt to satisfy needs at one stage or level until the needs at the lower stages are satisfied.

First, we are motivated to fulfill physiological needs. This includes food, water, shelter, and sleep for basic survival. After these needs are met, we are motivated by the desire to feel secure and safe from future dangers. When we prepare for future physiological needs, we are working proactively to satisfy our need for safety and security.

Next, we have our social-acceptance needs—the need to have friends and feel like we belong. When these needs are gratified, our concern shifts to self-esteem, the desire to develop self-respect, gain the approval of others, and achieve personal success. Now we have "self-actualization," right? Is this the highest level of Maslow's Hierarchy of Needs? No, it's not.

THE HIGHEST NEED LEVEL

Maslow's Hierarchy of Needs is illustrated in Figure 6. Note that self-actualization is not at the top. Maslow revised his renowned hierarchy shortly before his death in 1970, placing self-transcendence above self-actualization.[14] Transcending the self means going beyond self-interest to actively care for others.

It seems intuitive that various self-needs require satisfaction before self-transcendent or actively-caring-for-people (AC4P) behavior is likely to occur. But scant research supports the ranking of human needs in a hierarchy. It's possible to think of many examples of individuals performing various AC4P behaviors before satisfying all of their personal needs. Mahatma Gandhi put the concerns of others before his own. He suffered imprisonment, extensive fasts, and eventually assassination in his fifty-year struggle to help his poor and downtrodden compatriots.

Note the connection between the need hierarchy and various rewarding consequences, as well as our discussion of self-motivation and sustaining the impact of a behavior-improvement intervention. An individual's position in the hierarchy certainly determines what types of consequences are likely to be most

Figure 6: Maslow's revised hierarchy with self-transcendence at the top

rewarding at a particular time. Without food, shelter, or sleep, for example, most people will focus their efforts on satisfying these needs. But if this need level is satisfied, the motivation of human behavior requires consequences related to higher-level needs.

Note the connection between the need hierarchy and various rewarding consequences, as well as our discussion of self-motivation and sustaining the impact of a behavior-improvement intervention. An individual's position in the hierarchy certainly determines what types of consequences are likely to be most rewarding at a particular time. Without food, shelter, or sleep, for example, most people will focus their efforts on satisfying these needs. But if this need level is satisfied, the motivation of human behavior requires consequences related to higher-level needs.

As we climb Maslow's hierarchy, need states are reached that implicate consequences linked to self-motivation. For example, consequences that boost one's sense of connection with others (i.e., community) satisfy the need for acceptance or social support, and consequences that certify a person's belief in personal competence to perform worthwhile work are associated with the self-esteem and self-actualization needs. Plus, it's intuitive that reaching beyond self-needs to help others through AC4P behavior can contribute to satisfying a person's need for social acceptance and self-esteem, and even self-actualization.

Question: When does a person's need for social acceptance, self-esteem, and self-actualization get satisfied? In other words, at what point does a person become satiated on consequences linked to these need states? Yes, these are rhetorical questions, posed to reiterate the value of delivering rewarding consequences that reflect the three C-words of self-motivation (i.e., Competence, Choice, and Community) and enhance need states in Maslow's hierarchy that are difficult to satiate.

Bottom line: Behavioral consequences that foster perceptions of personal competence, self-worth, interpersonal belongingness, and/or autonomy also facilitate self-motivation and self-directed behavior, and are thus likely to have longer-term impact than consequences unrelated to these person-states.

Discussion Exercise

It would be helpful to discuss practical answers to the critical question implicated above: What kinds of behavioral consequences support or enhance your personal perceptions of choice, competence, and community on the job?

_____

_____

_____

_____

_____

In many cases, the verbal delivery of supportive feedback (as discussed earlier) can influence the recipient's self-motivation. Please specify below the verbal support you give to others or receive from others that benefit the C-words of self-motivation: Choice, Competence, and Community.

_____

_____

_____

_____

_____

THE AC4P MOVEMENT

Our Vision: A brother/sister keepers' culture in which everyone looks out for each other's safety and security—people routinely going above and beyond the call of duty to benefit the health, safety, and/or welfare of others.

We're talking about "Actively Caring for People"—AC4P. Most people care about the well-being of others, but relatively few "act" on their feelings of caring. The challenge: How can people be activated and motivated to *actively care*—to take effective AC4P action based on their caring.

AC4P policing contributes to this challenge and helps nurture interpersonal empathy, compassion, and AC4P behavior. Wearing the AC4P wristband signifies your support of the AC4P Movement. When you reward the desirable behavior of another person with an AC4P wristband, you promote and enhance the AC4P Movement.

Discussion Questions

1. What are some behaviors a police officer might observe from people in the community that warrant the reward of an AC4P wristband?

_____

_____

_____

_____

2. What would you say to the person when rewarding an AC4P behavior with an AC4P wristband?

_____

_____

_____

As we discussed earlier, you should specify the desirable AC4P behavior you observed and appreciate. Then you'd hand the wristband to the individual as recognition for setting an AC4P example. Deliver the wristband with words that serve a higher-level need. For example, never suggest or even imply that the wristband is a "pay-off" for AC4P behavior. Rather, the wristband is a token of appreciation for the "special servant leadership exemplified by the act of kindness I observed."

Tell the person s/he is now one of many who have joined the AC4P Movement—a flourishing worldwide effort to cultivate cultures of interpersonal compassion and interdependent AC4P behavior.

Then explain the SAPS Process: See, Act, Pass, Share, so the individual will continue the AC4P process. Specifically, tell the person to *See* a person looking out for the welfare of another individual. Then, *act* to recognize and reward this person for the AC4P behavior you saw by *passing* on the AC4P wristband "I just gave you".

Please ask this wristband recipient and new member of the AC4P Movement to *share* the positive police-citizen exchange on the Internet at www.ac4p.org by registering the number of the wristband, and briefly describe the AC4P behavior that led to the delivery of the AC4P wristband.

In this way, positive gossip is spread about police-citizen relations, and others see that behaving beyond one's self-interests on behalf of another person is more common than one might think. Such AC4P storytelling will contribute to making AC4P behavior a social norm and cultivate a culture of interpersonal trust, compassion, and routine AC4P behavior.

The SAPS process is much easier said than done. Why, because such behavior is not part of one's normal routine, and is not expected behavior, especially from a police officer. People do not normally look for desirable behavior to reward, even though this is the most powerful way to improve behavior (Lesson 1). In fact, people commonly deny even a "thank you" given for their kind act with expressions like, "No problem," "Don't worry about it," or "Just doing my job.

Receiving an AC4P wristband from a police officer should be a very rewarding and memorable experience. Whenever the AC4P concept is explained to others, it's always appreciated; and whenever an AC4P wristband is offered, it's always accepted with a sincere smile and worn with a sense of pride. We know many individuals who wear their AC4P wristband every day, and actually resist passing it on.

Now imagine an individual receiving an AC4P wristband from a police officer who gives a gracious and tactful description of the AC4P behavior that justified the recognition. Such rare and unexpected recognition from an officer of the law will surely be accepted with pleasant surprise. And will this wristband recipient tell friends and family of this very positive and special encounter with a police officer?

Yes, of course, and as these positive exchanges between law-enforcement officers and the citizens they serve accumulate, the media will most certainly pay attention and spread the good news about AC4P Policing. The AC4P Movement will spread throughout the community, and police officers will be identified as the agents of this research-based approach to promoting acts of kindness, relevant to preventing interpersonal conflict, abuse, and violence.

FEEDFORWARD AND THE SAPS PROCESS

The AC4P wristbands and SAPS process have been presented and discussed as essentially a feedback process for showing appreciation and rewarding the AC4P behavior of others.

Police officers look for AC4P behavior from citizens. When they observe such behavior, they seize the opportunity to reward that AC4P behavior and solicit another participant for the AC4P Movement. Question: How often do you have an opportunity to actually observe AC4P behavior in situations where it's convenient or at least feasible to deliver an AC4P wristband and the AC4P Movement message?

People have told us they do not readily observe AC4P behavior; and when they do, it's often not socially convenient or appropriate to reward that behavior on the spot. This might be particularly the case for police officers who spend most of their workdays serving others, rather than the reverse.

We find ourselves in situations daily where someone treats us or someone else with an act of kindness, and we can conveniently take an AC4P wristband off our wrist and pass it on. But this interactive process has taken practice, and we are often in environmental settings (e.g., on a university campus) where AC4P behavior is readily observable and relatively convenient to reward with an AC4P wristband. This might not be the case for many police officers.

Here's an alternative approach to distributing AC4P wristbands and promoting the AC4P Movement. Deliver the AC4P wristband as feedforward rather than feedback. Consider giving AC4P wristbands to citizens after you perform an AC4P behavior for them.

In other words, after a citizen thanks you for your AC4P behavior on behalf of his or her safety, security, or well-being, you follow up by passing on an AC4P wristband and a request to join the AC4P Movement. You might say something like:

Thank you for appreciating the positive behaviors performed by police officers. Wouldn't it be nice if all of us performed more acts of kindness on behalf of others? In fact, the police officers in our community have joined an Actively Caring for People initiative or AC4P Movement to spread positive interpersonal behavior nationwide, and actually worldwide. This wristband reflects this Movement and I hope you will wear it and join us.

Every wristband is engraved with its own ID number. I will record the ID number on the wristband I have given you when I report this AC4P event at the AC4P Policing Website. There is a citizen website for you to report my act of kindness, along with the ID number on your wristband. That Website address is engraved on the wristband, or you can use the abbreviation: ac4p.org.

Then I hope you will look for opportunities to pass on your wristband, either after you perform an act of kindness for another person, or when you see another person help someone else. In the first case, you are acknowledging your own act of kindness, as I did with you; in the second scenario, you are rewarding an individual for his or her AC4P behavior.

Of course, the quotation above is only a suggestion. You might certainly find another way to express three key points: 1) You explain why you passed on the AC4P wristband to the beneficiary of your AC4P service; 2) You introduce the AC4P Movement and the reporting of AC4P stories at two Websites, along with the ID number on the wristband; and 3) You encourage this new member of the AC4P Movement to pass on the wristband when s/he performs an act of kindness (as feedforward) or when s/he observes an AC4P act from another person (as feedback).

Discussion Question

After explaining this feedforward approach to passing on an AC4P wristband, it would be useful to discuss any perceived benefits of this process besides having an opportunity to explain the AC4P Movement and pass on an AC4P wristband.

In other words, how could this feedforward approach influence the occurrence of more AC4P behavior? We suggest you jot down some possibilities here, and then discuss the variety of answers among colleagues or workshop participants.

_____

_____

_____

_____

_____

_____

PSYCHOLOGICAL IMPACT OF FEEDFORWARD

Lessons 1 and 3 covered the rationale and benefits of rewarding people for their AC4P behavior. Simply put, such feedback can boost self-esteem, personal competence, and a sense of community or belongingness; and it increases the likelihood of that individual performing another act of kindness. Plus, you help that person "bask in the reflected glory" of reaching the highest level of Maslow's Hierarchy of Needs—self-transcendence (Lesson 7).

But what about the feedforward method? What is the psychological impact of you giving someone an AC4P wristband after you have helped that person?

It's possible your discussion above arrived at the same evidence-based advantages of the feedforward approach that we explain here. Often our own experiences inform us of human dynamics. Was this the case for you and/or your discussion group? To answer this rhetorical question, let's consider the social influence *Principle of Reciprocity.*

Social psychologists have provided much research evidence that many people feel a need, even an obligation, to pass on a good turn after receiving one from another person.[15] Whenever possible, the favor is returned to the original benefactor. But when this is impossible, as when a stranger contributes an AC4P behavior, the beneficiary of the kind act can satisfy the need to reciprocate by helping someone else, even a total stranger. Thus, the reciprocity norm and the related research suggest the AC4P feedforward wristband will influence the recipient to perform an AC4P act.

The social influence *Principle of Consistency* is also relevant here.[15] In particular, this research-supported principle indicates that people attempt to make their actions and attitudes consistent. As a result, it's possible to "act a person into a certain attitude (or way of thinking), and vice versa." Thus, whenever people perform an act of kindness and/or pass on an AC4P wristband, their positive thoughts and attitudes about the AC4P Movement get a boost.

Every time a police officer distributes an AC4P wristband as feedforward or as feedback a deposit is made in his/her attitudinal or emotional bank account for the AC4P Movement. S/he becomes more committed to the AC4P mission of building positive police-citizen relations and cultivating cultures of interpersonal compassion.

Relatedly, how could the principle of consistency influence the AC4P behaviors and attitudes of the recipient of a feedforward wristband? You know the answer, right? When accepting the wristband and putting it on (we hope), the individual is performing behaviors that reflect a positive attitude toward the AC4P Movement. If this person later logs on to the ac4p.org Website and reports his/her positive exchange with a police officer, more behavioral deposits are made to support positive self-talk, attitudes and affect toward the AC4P Movement.

Plus, this individual might receive supportive feedback regarding this website posting, since stories posted on the ac4p.org Website are forwarded to that individual's Facebook page. Such social support could serve as more Feedforward to influence more AC4P behavior.

Eventually the continual spiraling of interpersonal feedforward fueling AC4P behavior that is supported by interpersonal supportive feedback can result in genuine personal commitment to the AC4P Movement.

Discussion Questions
The instructor should facilitate interactive discussions of the following qzuestions, perhaps in small sub-groups and followed by reports to the entire audience.

1. What positive short-term and long-term consequences are likely if police officers are successful in spreading the AC4P Movement throughout their community? Note how answers to this question will serve to motivate individual and group execution of the AC4P Policing process (Lesson 1).

_____

_____

_____

_____

_____

_____

2. What is the value of recording each wristband delivery by a police officer on the Website: www.ac4ppolicing.org?

_____

_____

_____

_____

_____

_____

3. How could police officers be "motivated" to record their SAPS experiences on the AC4P Policing Website?

_____

_____

_____

_____

_____

_____

_____

4. What factors might hold one back from initiating and maintaining the SAPS process? How could these potential barriers be minimized?

_____

_____

_____

_____

_____

_____

5. What support is needed from the community to guarantee the large-scale success of AC4P Policing?

_____

_____

_____

_____

_____

_____

6. Is there more to AC4P Policing than the SAPS process? Please explain.

_____

_____

_____

_____

_____

_____

_____

7. What are the most important take-a-ways from this education/training program? In other words, what principles and/or procedures covered in this program were most useful to you?

_____

_____

_____

_____

_____

_____

8. In what ways are the principles applied in AC4P Policing useful beyond your job? In other words, how might you apply these principles or procedures in situations other than AC4P Policing?

_____

_____

_____

_____

_____

_____

9. What did you like best about this education/training program?

_____

_____

_____

_____

_____

_____

_____

10. How could this education/training for AC4P Policing be improved?

_____

_____

_____

_____

_____

_____

_____

ROLE PLAYING EXERCISE

This final role-playing exercise is most critical. Specifically, participants should have an opportunity to practice the interpersonal communication steps of delivering an AC4P wristband as both feedforward and feedback, and explaining the SAPS process.

This could be accomplished by the participants pairing off and playing the role of "giver" and "receiver" of a feedforward and feedback delivery of an AC4P wristband. Subsequently, volunteers could "replay" their interactions before the entire group of participants, followed by feedback from the instructor and other observers.

Alternatively, the participants could stay with their discussion groups and develop a role-play demonstration for the entire group. It would be enjoyable and perhaps instructive to create a role play of the wrong and right ways to deliver and receive an AC4P wristband as feedforward and feedback.

The purpose: to help participants feel comfortable giving people an AC4P wristband as feedforward and feedback, and explaining the SAPS process. Yes, this is easier said than done, but participation should be motivated by realizing the various positive consequences of a successful AC4P Policing process.

CONCLUSION

Congratulations! You have just learned leading-edge principles and procedures for improving other people's behavior, while also increasing positive connections between you, your colleagues, and the citizens you serve.

We sincerely hope you have acquired more than an *understanding* of the seven principles of humanistic behaviorism (the academic term for the foundation of AC4P Policing), but that you *believe* in the validity of these research-based principles for improving interpersonal attitudes and behavior related to cultivating an AC4P culture.

Most importantly, we hope you feel *empowered* to begin practicing the principles with family members, colleagues, and eventually the citizens you serve in the community. For example, implementing the feedforward and feedback techniques with empathy will surely reap observable benefits. Plus, by reflecting on the results of your behavior-focused conversations you will continuously improve your skills at benefitting other people's behavior through one-to-one conversation.

Then, when you add the AC4P wristband and the SAPS process to your communications with the citizens you serve, you maximize the positive consequences of each conversation. You will have recruited another participant for the AC4P Movement, and thus helped to nurture an AC4P culture of interpersonal trust, empathy, compassion, and routine acts of kindness.

The result: Police officers will be viewed as positive proactive agents of beneficial change rather than as negative law-enforcement officials who only react to antisocial behavior or crises with punitive consequences.

SUGGESTED READINGS

Biglan, A. (2015). *The nurture effect: How the science of human behavior can improve our lives and our world.* Oakland, CA: New Harbinger Publications, Inc.

Geller, E.S. (2016) (Ed.). *Actively caring for people: Cultivating a culture of compassion* (5th Edition). Newport, VA: Make-A-Difference, LLC.

Geller, E.S. (2016) (Ed.). *Applied psychology: Actively caring for people.* New York: Cambridge University Press.

NOTES

1. E. Scott Geller, Alumni Distinguished Professor, and Director, Center for Applied Behavior Systems, Virginia Tech, Blacksburg, VA. Email: esgeller@vt.edu.

2. Bobby Kipper, Director, National Center for the Prevention of Community Violence (NCPCV) Email: bobbykipper@solveviolence.com.

3. Geller, E.S., & Kipper, B. (2015). AC4P Policing: A research-based process for cultivating positive police-community relations. *Police Chief,* September, p. 41.

4. Geller, E.S. (2016) (Ed.). *Actively caring for people: Cultivating a culture of compassion* (5th Edition). Newport, VA: Make-A-Difference, LLC; Geller,E.S. (2016) (Ed.). *Applied Psychology: Actively caring for people.* New York: Cambridge University Press.

5. Geller, E.S. (2016). Seven life lessons from humanistic behaviorism: How to bring the best out of yourself and others. *Journal of Organizational Behavior Management,* 35(1), 151-170

6. Carnegie, D. (1936). *How to win friends and influence people* (1981 Edition), New York: Simon and Schuster, p. 19.

7. Bandura, A. (1969). *Principles of behavior modification.* New York: Holt, Reinhold & Winston.

8. Dweck, C.S. (2006). *Mindset: The new psychology of success.* New York: Ballantine Books.

9. Chance, P. (2008). *The teacher's craft: The 10 essential skills of effective teaching.* Long Grove, IL: Waveland Press, Inc.; Reed, D. et al. (2016). Actively caring for higher education. In E.S. Geller (Ed). *Applied psychology: Actively caring for people* (pp.563-593). New York: Cambridge University Press.

10. Thorndike, E.L. (1931). *Human learning.* Cambridge, MA: MIT Press.

11. Carnegie, D. (1936). *How to win friends and influence people* (1981 Edition), New York: Simon and Schuster.

12. Covey, S.R. (1989). *The seven habits of highly effective people* New York: Simon and Schuster.

13. Deci, E.L., & Flaste, R. (1995). *Why we do what we do: Understanding self-motivation.* New York: Penguin Books; Geller, E.S. (2016). The psychology of self-motivation. In Geller, E.S. (Ed.). *Applied psychology: Actively caring for people* (pp.83-118). New York: Cambridge University Press; Geller, E.S., & Veazie, R.A. (2010). *When no one's watching: Living and leading self-motivation.* Newport, VA: Make-A-Difference, LLC.

14. Maslow, A.H. (1971). *The farther reaches of human nature* New York: Viking.

15. Cialdini, R.B. (2001). *Influence: Science and practice* (6th edition). Boston, MA: Pearson Education; Furrow, C., & Geller, E.S. (2016). Social influence and AC4P behavior. In E.S. Geller (Ed.). *Applied psychology: Actively caring for people* (pp. 185-227), New York: Cambridge University Press.

AC4P POLICING IN ACTION

In the Fall of 2015, six police agencies across America learned about the AC4P principles and began to apply AC4P Policing. These departments and their leadership are indeed the pioneers of AC4P Policing in the U.S. In fact, their successful applications of the AC4P principles inspired the preparation and publication of this training manual. We are indebted to these organizations for convincing us that AC4P Policing is a practical and socially valid process for cultivating and nourishing positive relations between police officers and the citizens they serve. The result: more communitywide collaboration for interpersonal safety, national security, and world peace. These innovative AC4P police departments are as follows:

- Winter Park Police Department, Winter Park, FL
- Richton Park Police Department, Richton Park, IL
- Prescott Police Department, Prescott, AZ
- Coolidge Police Department, Coolidge, AZ
- Flagstaff Police Department, Flagstaff, AZ
- Norfolk Police Department, Norfolk, VA

Plus, we owe a special "thanks" to the Florida Police Chiefs Association for becoming the first Police Chief's Association in America to adopt AC4P Policing as a community policing process.

TESTIMONIES FROM LEADERS OF AC4P POLICING

We have received the following testimonies from leaders of the innovative police organizations who have already observed the benefits of AC4P Policing.

Being a cop is a calling. Most who join the ranks of our history are intrinsically motivated to protect and serve. This career of community service calls for a life-changing mindset, one which compels my officers to place their lives on the line to ensure our communities are safe. Although I value each and every one of my officers for their dedication and professionalism, the great deeds they accomplish on a daily basis are commonly unnoticed by media highlights.

AC4P has provided my officers and the community members we serve with immediate recognition of the goodness that derives from our daily interactions. Although the Norfolk Police Department is involved in continual community outreach initiatives, AC4P brings something unique to the table. It has allowed for immediate community engagement. My officers witness an act of kindness or a moment of caring, and the reward is instantaneous. The story is shared and the positive exchanges between people are highlighted through a "pay it forward" mentality. I'm confident my officers already had an "actively caring" mindset, but now they're helping to cultivate an actively-caring culture throughout their community.

AC4P brings us back to the grassroots effort of interpersonal communication, and by its very nature, develops the positive police-community interactions we all want to see.

—**Chief Michael G. Goldsmith**,
Norfolk Police Department, Norfolk, VA

It is my firm belief that there is nothing so important to effective law enforcement today than the establishment of public trust. One of the most effective ways to establish public trust is through the development of relationships and partnerships. AC4P policing assists agencies in this pursuit.

It allows a law enforcement agency to place itself in a position where good behavior is recognized. It allows officers to make contact with our citizens to celebrate the positive.

Here's a personal example I observed not long after our agency adopted AC4P Policing. The city of Flagstaff is a community of 68,000 citizens located in Northern Arizona. It is also home to the Northern Arizona University, a campus of over 20,000 students. Like many college towns, our police department responds to its share of college parties and student indiscretion. As a 29 year veteran, I have had more than my share of negative contacts with college students. Thus, the relationship between City police and students can often be strained and sometimes adverse.

I was actually contemplating our negative connections with college students when driving by the northern border of our University last summer. As I approached a four-way stop, I saw a college student standing in the middle of the intersection to my right. He was just standing there, blocking the road. As vehicles were stopping and going, I moved closer and closer to this student, and I became more and more frustrated with what appeared to be his complete indignation for the traffic laws. He just continued to stand in the middle of the intersection. All traffic in front of me and other points at the four-way stop were headed different directions, so no one drove toward the student.

When I finally reached the intersection, I had seen enough. I grabbed by badge as I was in plain clothes, pulled to the side of the road, jumped out and identified myself to the student. I then asked the obvious question, "Why are you standing in the middle of the street?" I did my best to hide my disgust, but I don't doubt he might have had just a hint I was upset. He simply pointed with his thumb over his shoulder.

I looked behind him down the street from where he was standing and I saw an ambulance and fire truck, as well as one of our police cars blocking the street. A motorcyclist was down from an obvious collision and receiving treatment. I had not heard the call on my radio as I had just left the station located about one minute from this traffic crash. The student had taken it upon himself to conduct traffic control in the middle of the roadway in order to prevent cars from driving toward the collision.

Well I felt pretty small, but was immediately vindicated when I grabbed a green colored AC4P bracelet from my car and presented it to him. I briefly explained the AC4P Movement, shook his hand, and told him how proud I was he took the initiative to assist our first responders. I gave him an AC4P thank-you card, took his name and drove off as other officers arrived to take over his duties.

The young man contacted me three weeks later to explain he was a pre-med student graduating that summer. He asked if he could use my name as a reference on his application to medical school. I happily obliged.

For me this scenario illustrates the opportunity of AC4P Policing to establish positive interpersonal relations and break down barriers to positive collaboration. I am convinced of its potential to benefit law enforcement.

—Chief Kevin Treadway,
Flagstaff Police Department, Flagstaff, AZ

Police departments all across our country are always looking for ways to connect the communities they serve in a positive way. The principles of community policing still hold true today as they did years ago when first introduced. AC4P Policing is all about human behavior and promoting positive interactions between the law enforcement community and the people it serves. AC4P Policing exemplifies the foundations of community policing and helps promote civility, respect for others, and adds to the quality of life in communities that embrace it.

Plus, AC4P Policing is a process in line with President Obama's Task Force on 21st Century Policing. As mentioned in the final report of this task force, dated May 2015, under Pillar 4, "Community Policing requires the active building of positive relationships with members of the community." AC4P Policing does just that.

—**Chief Jerald Monahan**,
Prescott Police Department, Prescott, AZ
Past President of the Board of Directors for the
Arizona Association of Chiefs of Police

In late 2015, Winter Park Police Chief Brett Railey, the president of the Florida Police Chiefs Association (FPPCA), told me about the success he was seeing in Winter Park after implementing the AC4P Policing process. One of the FPCA's goals is to help our member agencies develop positive relationships within their communities, and AC4P Policing is a natural fit.

We introduced AC4P Policing to our members at our Winter Conference in January 2016, and we became the first association of our kind to formally endorse the process. Special blue AC4P wristbands were created for our members to support police officer colors, and we invited our members to a training session on how to implement AC4P Policing. Far too often, we hear stories about negative police-citizen interactions in their communities. We are committed to changing this narrative, and we believe the AC4P Policing process is an excellent tool to make that happen. We want to see this process spread throughout our entire state, and thereby promote good news of positive interactions between police officers and the citizens they serve.

—**Amy Mercer**, Executive Director of the
Florida Police Chiefs Association

AC4P POLICING STORIES FROM THE FIELD

As detailed in this education/training manual, the AC4P Policing process includes the delivery of a special AC4P wristband from police officer to citizen under two positive situations: Feedforward and Feedback. A feedforward delivery of an AC4P wristband occurs when a citizen expresses gratitude following a police officer's assistance. Alternatively, police officers use the AC4P wristband to reward citizens for acts of kindness they see them perform. This serves as supportive feedback to encourage recurrence of such AC4P behavior. Police officers record their feedforward and feedback interactions at the Website: www.ac4ppolicing.org. Eight representative feedback stories are included here. The feedforward approach had not been explained to these police departments.

On February 21, 2016, I pulled up behind two vehicles stopped on the side of the road, one behind the other. At first I thought there had been a minor accident, but then it became apparent that the first vehicle, a white van, was disabled. When I walked up to the van, I saw a young man in a Navy sweatshirt and jeans underneath the van working a jack. This man's name is Jevon Smith and according to the driver of the van, Douglas Faley, he was a stranger who had pulled over to help him.

The van's tire had actually fallen off due to a few missing lug nuts. Smith used his own jack from his car as the van's jack was not working properly. Smith assisted Foley in recovering the tire and re-installing it, then going as far as to make sure the other three tires were secure as well. Smith was out with his girlfriend and three-month old baby son, who was sleeping peacefully in his car seat. Smith should be commended for his actions as he was out enjoying a beautiful afternoon with his son and girlfriend, but stopped in order to render assistance to a fellow citizen. Smith currently serves in the U.S. Navy on the Mesa Verde LPD 19. I gave Jevon Smith Green Wristband #115,710.

—**Officer M. Pierce**,
Norfolk Police Department, Norfolk, VA.

On February 10, 2016, officers from the Norfolk Police Department responded to a call for service for a teenager who had jumped from the

Campostella Bridge into the Lafayette River approximately 70 feet below. Upon arrival by officers, the teenager had already removed himself from the water and was standing on a small dock in the middle of the river. The dock was not accessible by any other means than the water. The teenager was soaking wet and enduring 40 degree weather with high winds and unknown injuries from the fall.

While officers on the scene coordinated a rescue effort, three men, Christian Crabtree, Boyce "Russell" Orr, and Bryen Lindsey operating a small tugboat recognized the occurring situation and maneuvered their boat next to the dock and safely brought the teenager aboard. After bringing him to dry land, the three men were able to transfer the young man to awaiting officers and paramedics. Thanks to the quick and decisive action by these three men the teenager was safely brought to Norfolk General Hospital and is recovering with his family. Green Wristbands #125158, #125153, and #125134 were given to these three heroes.

—**Officers F. St. George and T. M. Gimber**,
Norfolk Police Department

On Jan 2, 2016 I was dispatched to a burglary in progress. When I arrived at the scene, Mr. Hull was standing outside waiting for police to arrive in order to give an accurate description on the suspect. Mr. Hull stated that he believes community citizens should stick together and watch out for each other. Due to his quick action and accurate description, the suspect was apprehended. Mr. Hull's actions showed that when people come together positive change can be made. He accepted Wristband #125047.

—**K. Boone**, Norfolk Police Department, Norfolk, VA.

On 1/12/16 at approximately 3:45 pm while on patrol, I observed a U.S. Navy member at the intersection of Tidewater Drive and Virginia Beach Blvd. pushing a car out of the intersection by himself after the car had run out of gas. Since this is a very busy time for vehicle traffic the military member acted quickly with his assistance. The military member's name is Petty Officer First Class Matthew K. Smeltekop. The military member stayed behind to ensure that the driver had a way to get some gas. He received Wristband #126073.

—**Officer T. Hardesty**,
Norfolk Police Department, Norfolk, VA.

On December 15th I was dispatched to a call for service at 1300 Longdale Dr. #101 to recover a wallet found by Ron White. I spoke with Mr. White, the resident of Apt. 101, who informed me the wallet was found in the parking lot of the complex. He was concerned because it had the personal information of the owner, as well as $226 dollars in cash.

Mr. White should be recognized for his integrity and due diligence for his act of honesty. I presented Mr. White with an AC4P wristband (#126312) and explained the AC4P Movement. He was very receptive and thanked me for my service. It was a pleasure talking with Mr. White, and I hope others who read this story will follow his example.

—**Officer Palevich**,
Norfolk Police Department, Norfolk, VA.

While sitting in the briefing room, I observed two of our records clerks walking by. They were pulling a cart of copying paper. I also observed officers engaged in conversation while watching the records clerks struggling with the cart. An explorer who was speaking with me, excused himself from the conversation and went and assisted the records clerks.

It was awesome to watch this young man react the way he did. I then explained the AC4P Movement to him, and how it's about paying it forward with acts of kindness. His reaction to receiving the wristband (#122357) was priceless.

The officers who had observed the young man's AC4P behavior listened intently to my explanation of the Movement. They surely thought about the act of kindness they saw, as well as their missed opportunity to pay it forward. I believe change first starts within, and then one can see what needs to be done.

—**Commander Rodney Smith**,
Coolidge Police Department, Coolidge, AZ.

On October 16, 2015, while on patrol I decided to take a break at the local Subway restaurant. When approaching the cashier, I learned someone had already paid for my meal. I spoke with "Nicole" and thanked her for her kindness. "Nicole" told me she lives for the pay-it -forward experience, and wants to do good in this world. Her husband advised me that she is always doing these kinds of things and is one of the genuinely good people on this world. Encounters like this remind me of the kind nature of people. I was so pleased to give her wristband #122156.

—**W.L. Hoyle**,
Coolidge Police Department, Coolidge, AZ.

Officer Javier Rodriguez responded to an elementary school in Winter Park to assist the administration with a parent and two children who were homeless and in need of assistance. Officer Rodriguez spent hours calling every shelter and organization he could think of in an attempt to get their mother some assistance and a place to stay. When he was unable to find a shelter that could accommodate this mom and her two children, Officer Rodriguez reached into his own pocket and gave the woman eighty dollars to help her, and also found a friend of hers who was willing to take her in for the night. Officer Rodriguez received wristband #130707 for his actively caring for people.

—**Officer Javier Rodriguez**,
Winter Park Police Department, Winter Park, FL.

Sergeant Errol Colon recognized David Hahn for providing assistance to two female drivers who were involved in a traffic crash, within the area of S. Orlando Avenue and New England Avenue. Upon arriving on the scene of the traffic crash, Sergeant Colon noticed Mr. Hahn providing aide to both female drivers who were visibly upset from the crash. Once determined that no injuries to either of the females was sustained, Mr. Hahn walked back to his place of business, the Italio restaurant, and returned with cold bottled water for all of the officers on scene as well as for the females involved within the crash.

Sergeant E. Colon recognized Mr. Hahn with wristband #127011 for his kindness and active actions to care for the females involved in the traffic crash, and for his thoughtfulness to bring water to the officers on scene.

—**Sergeant Errol Colon**,
Winter Park Police Department, Winter Park, FL.

At approximately 1930 hours, Officer Reneski came into contact with Mr. Glenn Miller at WaWa gas station located at 901 North Orlando Avenue. Mr. Miller advised he pulled up to a fuel pump and found an iPhone and he wanted to do the right thing and return the phone to the owner, but was unsure how to do that. I advised he could wait and the owner would most likely call the phone.

While waiting at WaWa, the owner did call the phone and Mr. Miller advised he would wait at the current location to meet with the owner and return the phone. I recognized Mr. Miller for his actions in actively caring for another person and their property with wristband #131624. Mr. Miller showed a true act of kindness in making sure a complete stranger received their valuable lost property instead of taking it for his own gain.

—**Officer Reneski**,
Winter Park Police Department, Winter Park, FL.

On a recent spring morning in April, a man wandered into the Police Administration Building in Downtown Norfolk. The man smiled politely with a wide, toothy grin and stared at the officers. When asked if he needed any assistance, the man simply stated, "I think I'm lost."

The man knew his first name and believed he was married. He recalled living in Connecticut in the 1970's and was dressed in newer clothing with shoe soles that hadn't been worn through miles of walking. Without a wallet or identification cards, a cell phone would have surely shed light on family contacts. As he pulled his hands from his jean pockets, a few strands of lint fell from the lining. His hands were empty and officers were left with a 60-year-old man, whose memory ended in 1975.

Thankfully, out of all the buildings in Downtown Norfolk, the man managed to open the one wooden door located under a small, blue awning. Behind the door were the Chief of Police and his officers ready to assist. One hour later, police radios could still be heard broadcasting the lost man's description in hopes of finding family.

After scouring the Downtown streets, a woman was located outside the Battleship Wisconsin. A worried wife was comforted with the knowledge her loved one was found as officers reunited the family.

The officers involved in searching for the man's family received AC4P Wristbands #126779, #126772, and #126778. Each officer took the time to comfort the man, during what can only be assumed as an extremely stressful event for a person suffering from cognitive ailments or dementia.

The personal attention this man and his family received was above the call of duty. They treated the lost soul and his wife with the respect that you'd want for your own grandparents, and in turn, provided a happy ending for what could have been a tragic outcome.

Kudos to the officers and the Norfolk Police Department for their daily efforts in excellence.

—**Melinda Wray**,
Public Information Officer, Norfolk, VA.

On April 4th, 2016 I responded to an accident on Sewell's Pt Rd where a car had pulled out in front of a motorcycle, causing an accident. A good Samaritan who saw the accident stopped, checked on the injured motorcyclist, called 911, and stayed on scene until paramedics and PD arrived to make sure that the motorcyclist was ok. This good Samaritan choose to stay and help not only the victim but PD as well instead of just driving by as many others had. I thanked him for his help and kindness and awarded him AC4P Wristband #125076 for his selfless act.

—Officer Christopher Deuell,
Norfolk Police Department, Norfolk, VA.

SUMMARY

As evident from these testimonies and wristband stories, the AC4P Policing story in America is being told through the actions of the officers referenced above, and by countless other police professionals who are now embracing this new positive approach to citizen-centered policing. Even before this AC4P Policing education/training manual had been published, several additional police departments have joined the Movement. The stories here provide only a glimpse of AC4P Policing and its positive consequences. Many more inspirational testimonies and AC4P stories are yet to come.

ABOUT THE AUTHORS

 **E. Scott Geller**, Ph.D. is an Alumni Distinguished Professor in the Department of Psychology at Virginia Tech. For more than four decades, Professor Geller has taught and conducted research as a faculty member and director of the Center for Applied Behavior Systems in the Department of Psychology. He has authored, edited or co-authored 36 books, 82 book chapters, 39 training programs, 259 magazine articles, and more than 300 research articles addressing the development and evaluation of behavior change interventions to improve quality of life on a large scale. His most recent book: *Applied Psychology: Actively Caring for People*, defines Dr. Geller's research, teaching, and scholarship career at Virginia Tech, which epitomizes the VT logo: *Ut Prosim* "That I May Serve".

Dr. Geller is a Fellow of the American Psychological Society, the Association for Psychological Science, the Association of Behavior Analysis International, and the World Academy of Productivity and Quality Sciences. He is past Editor of the *Journal of Applied Behavior Analysis* (1989-1992), current Associate Editor of *Environment and Behavior* (since 1982), and current Consulting Editor for *Behavior and Social Issues*, the *Journal of Organizational Behavior Management, and* the *Journal of Safety Research.*

Scott Geller's dedication, talent, and energy have helped him earn a teaching award in 1982 from the American Psychological Association and every university teaching award offered at Virginia Tech. In 2005, he was awarded the statewide Virginia Outstanding Faculty Award by the State Council of Higher Education, and Virginia Tech conferred the title of Alumni Distinguished Professor on him.

He has received lifetime achievement awards from the International Organizational Behavior Management Network (in 2008) and the American Psychological Foundation (in 2009). In 2011, the College of Wooster awarded Dr. Geller the Honorary Degree: Doctor of Humane letter.

Bobby Kipper began his career with the Newport News Police Department in 1977. During his 25-year career he served in the areas of patrol, investigations, media relations, and as executive assistant to the Chief of Police. Following his decorated 25 years' service with the department, he served as the director of Virginia's Gang Reduction Program at the Office of the Attorney General.

Mr. Kipper is the founder and director of the National Center for the Prevention of Community Violence. His expertise in the area of community and school violence prevention has been recognized by the White House, Congress, and a number of states across America. His best-selling book, *No Colors: 100 Ways to Keep Gangs from Taking Away Our Communities*, has been instrumental in developing gang reduction programs in communities across America.

In addition, Bobby Kipper has developed and presented a number of courses for the University of North Florida, Institute of Police Technology and Management; University of Memphis, Mid-South Training Institute; and the International Association of Chiefs of Police in the key areas of prevention and organizational leadership. His current best-selling book, *Performance Driven Thinking*, is serving as a new direction for public safety leadership in America.

Bobby has been awarded with the F.B.I. Director's Award for the fight against crime in America. In addition, during his police career he was recognized on three separate occasions with the Outstanding Contribution to Law Enforcement Award.

A free eBook edition is available with the purchase of this book.

To claim your free eBook edition:

1. Download the Shelfie app.
2. Write your name in upper case in the box.
3. Use the Shelfie app to submit a photo.
4. Download your eBook to any device.

Shelfie

A free eBook edition is available
with the purchase of this print book.

CLEARLY PRINT YOUR NAME ABOVE IN UPPER CASE

Instructions to claim your free eBook edition:
1. Download the Shelfie app for Android or iOS
2. Write your name in **UPPER CASE** above
3. Use the Shelfie app to submit a photo
4. Download your eBook to any device

Print & Digital Together Forever.

Snap a photo   Free eBook   Read anywhere

The Morgan James
Speakers Group

Morgan James makes all of our titles available
through the Library for All Charity Organizations.

www.LibraryForAll.org

CPSIA information can be obtained
at www.ICGtesting.com
Printed in the USA
JSHW070336020223
37180JS00008B/510